LIMITLESS ABIDING BIBLE STUDY

Shelly Funk and Stephanie Fleming

New Harbor Press

RAPID CITY, SD

Funk and Fleming/New Harbor Press
1601 Mt.Rushmore Rd, Ste 3288
Rapid City, SD 57701
www.newharborpress.com

Limitless Abiding Bible Study / Shelly Funk and Stephanie Fleiming. -- 1st ed.
ISBN 978-1-63357-414-4

CONTENTS

INTRODUCTION...1

CHAPTER 1: ABIDE 5

   LESSON 1: WHAT IS ABIDING?..6

   LESSON 2: HOW DO WE ABIDE?...11

      SECTION 1: BEING INTENTIONAL 11

      SECTION 2: ACTION STEPS 13

      SECTION 3: BUT WAIT, THERE'S MORE! 18

      SECTION 4: ATTACHING TO THE VINE.....................23

   LESSON 3: WHAT HAPPENS WHEN WE ABIDE?............25

CHAPTER 2: FRUIT OF THE SPIRIT 31

   LESSON 1: WHAT IS THE FRUIT OF THE SPIRIT?..........32

   LESSON 2: LOVE..36

   LESSON 3: JOY 39

   LESSON 4: PEACE..43

   LESSON 5: PATIENCE 47

   LESSON 6: KINDNESS...50

   LESSON 7: GOODNESS 52

   LESSON 8: FAITHFULNESS 56

   LESSON 9: GENTLENESS 60

   LESSON 10: SELF-CONTROL..65

CHAPTER 3: WAITING...71

   LESSON 1: REASONS FOR WAITING 72

      SECTION 1: RESTING 72

      SECTION 2: EXPECTING ANSWERS 74

SECTION 3: CHANGES..77
LESSON 2: WHAT WE GAIN FROM WAITING.................79
LESSON 3: WHAT TO DO WHILE WE WAIT 82
BIBLIOGRAPHY 89

INTRODUCTION

Abide.

Such a small word with such a huge meaning. It is a word that we, as Christians, hear in abundance. Have you ever really stopped to think about the word *abide*? I had not put much thought into that simple word until one ordinary day in 2020. Stephanie and I were having our usual Bible study at our usual Backyard Burger, in our usual booth, with our usual bacon cheeseburger meal. However, on this very ordinary day, the word ABIDE hit me in an extraordinary way. We refer to this type of hit as "God's holy freight train." On that day, the Holy Spirit inserted the concept of abiding deep into my soul and that simple word suddenly had new meaning and new depth. Stephanie and I began to really dig in and study abiding in Christ. We have since gleaned a much deeper understanding of how abiding is directly related to our relationship with Christ and how that relationship changes every aspect of daily living. It is no longer just a word I hear or read about in the Bible. It is a way of life!

After several months of the "abiding" obsession, the Holy Spirit pressed upon me to write a study guide for others. I pray that you, as you work through the study guide, will become obsessed as well.

—Shelly

I remember that day vividly. It wasn't the first time we had been run over by God's holy freight train, but it certainly was different from before! Shelly and I looked at each other in shock as we were able to understand *abiding* in a completely new way. After that, the word *abide* became our focus. It became more than just a word to me; it started to become a way of life. As we began to dig deeper and deeper into that word, Jesus showed me how free I can be when I abide in Him.

I never knew such a small word would have such a major impact on my life, but I can't deny the positive changes I'm seeing! God shows me all the time how much He works in my life when I abide. I can see His influence in more situations in my life than I ever had before. Unpacking that simple word has drawn me closer to Jesus, and I will never complain about that! My desire to abide in Him daily has grown exponentially.

As you work through this study, I pray that you would be open to the prompting of the Holy Spirit and allow yourself to be drawn closer to Him each day.

—Stephanie

A Note from Us

Throughout this study, we are going to be sharing some personal stories as well as stories from the Bible. We will be digging into Bible verses. We will also be asking you to do some introspection in our "thought spots" throughout the book. Our purpose is to help you enrich and deepen your relationship with Christ.

We are praying for you, friend. As a matter of fact, we prayed for you before we started writing and will continue to do so. We wrote this study with you in mind, not because we are experts or perfect in our own walks with Jesus, but because we want to share this journey with you. We have learned so much about abiding as we researched, and God convicted us in several areas of our lives as we wrote. There were many holy freight train moments! We have taken great joy in this process but also shed many tears. We wrote this book prayerfully and we wholeheartedly believe we wrote with the guidance of the Holy Spirit. We ask that you take your time and allow the Holy Spirit to reveal Himself and His desires for you.

Before you begin, say the following prayer, or pray your own prayer.

Heavenly Father, You are an awesome God. Thank You for the time to study Your Word and grow in my relationship with You. You promise in James 1:5 that if I ask for wisdom, You will give it generously. Lord, please give me Your wisdom and reveal Your truth as I work through this guide and read the Scriptures. Show me how to fully abide in You every day.
In Jesus' name, I pray, Amen.

CHAPTER 1

ABIDE

As human beings, we are born seekers. We are hard-wired to desire close connections. Whether it be a romantic relationship, a friendship, a familial relationship, or a spiritual relationship, we are designed to seek out those types of bonds. If we are honest, we are all longing for a relationship where we are understood and accepted. When we don't feel connected, we sometimes try to force connections with others in the wrong way or with the wrong people.

What if we told you the connection you seek is readily available to you? What if you did not have to rely on people or things to fulfill your relational needs? Can you imagine such a relationship?

We are not trying to sell you a quick self-help fix or a miracle cure. We want to help you see that the relationship you so desire is a relationship with Jesus. God made us to seek HIM. But so often, we misunderstand that desire as a physical need that can be met in the natural world.

The bad news is that nothing here on Earth can fill that need. There is no job, relationship, object, or substance that can provide us with all that we require. Likewise, the good news is that nothing here on Earth can fill that need. The best news is this: **Jesus has the ability and the desire to satisfy us completely**!

There is more to being a Christian than just believing and confessing. We need to enter into a "partnership" with God the Father.

This is where abiding enters the picture.

Lesson 1: What Is Abiding?

Before we get started on our journey, take a moment to consider our topic of study. What do you think of when you hear the word *abide* or the phrase *abiding in Christ*?

_____

_____

_____

_____

According to Dictionary.com, the definition of *abide* is as follows: (1) to remain; continue; stay; (2) to have one's abode; dwell; reside; (3) to continue in a particular condition, attitude, relationship, etc.; last.

Those definitions can easily apply to our relationship with Christ. We remain in Him. We dwell and reside in Him. We continue in Him. Did you catch all that? Read those sentences again, adding extra emphasis on the word IN. Seriously. Read them again.

We do not just hang out with Him, but we remain IN Him. As a matter of fact, this is exactly what He asks us to do in the Bible.

Look at John 15:10, "If you keep My commands, you will **remain in My** love, just as I have kept My Father's commands and **remain in** His love" (NIV; emphasis added).

The King James Version puts it this way: "If ye keep My commandments, ye shall **abide in** My love; even as I have kept My Father's commandments, and **abide in** His love" (emphasis added).

Jesus is telling us to abide in His love. Have you ever stopped to think about what He means by that statement? We believe He is telling us to remain, stay, and continue in His love and in a relationship with Him, which matches definition one of *abide*. Jesus doesn't want us to walk away from Him and His love for us.

Stop here and take some time to think about your relationship with God as it is right now. Can you say that you truly remain, stay, and continue in Him all day, every day? If not, how do you envision your relationship with Him chaning if you spend more time in His presence? What about your life? How would your life change if you spent more time with Him?

_____

_____

_____

_____

I (Shelly) have a strong testimony to how abiding has changed my life and my relationship with God. There were many years that I considered myself a Christian, but I didn't have a real connection with Christ. I struggled through life, making my own decisions, and trying to do it all on my own. I prayed. But that was the extent of my commitment. Needless to say, my life was a train wreck. I had a failed marriage, meaningless relationships, jobs I hated, and not enough money to pay my bills and eat. Sure, I asked God for help. However, I didn't give Him any of my time or any control over my life. Once I started spending time in the Word and finding ways to seek His face, everything turned around. I now have a great husband, a job I love, unexpected family connections, and more blessings than I deserve.

And even if things get difficult, I always feel God's presence and see Him working.

So, what if the answer to all our problems is to change our focus and let God have our lives? John 10:10 says, "The thief comes only to steal and kill and destroy. I came that they may have life and have it abundantly." John was telling us that when we do change our focus and let God have our lives, He promises to give us abundant life. Sounds pretty good, doesn't it? Since that is the answer, then how do we tap into this abundant life? Simple. Abide.

The second definition of *abide* means to "have one's abode." An abode is where someone resides and lives. It is where we spend our life. Home is our permanent dwelling place. Think about the building of a physical home. When a house is built, the solid rock (concrete) foundation is constructed first. No one would build a home or buy a home that is built on sand without a solid foundation. If we build our house on or abide in something other than Jesus, it is like building a house on the sand with no rock foundation.

Read Matthew 7:24–27, "Therefore everyone who hears these words of Mine and puts them into practice is like a wise man who built his house on the rock. The rain came down, the streams rose, and the winds blew and beat against that house, yet it did not fall, because it had its foundation on the rock. But everyone who hears these words of Mine and does not put them into practice is like a foolish man who built his house on sand. The rain came down, the streams rose, and the winds blew and beat against that house, and it fell with a great crash."

Notice how verses 24 and 26 mention putting God's Word into practice. It's not enough to just hear or read the Word. One of the ways we build our house on the Rock is that we must *put His Word into practice*, meaning we have to do what God asks of us. James 1:22 tells us, "But be **doers of the word** and not hearers only, deceiving yourselves" (emphasis added). Because He asks us to make Him our home, that is what we need to do. He wants to be our permanent shelter and dwelling of safety.

We are going to ask you to stop and think again. What foundation is your heart built on? It is very important to be honest with yourself here. Are you standing sturdy on the Rock or are you shakily trying to hold it together on the sand?

To say that my (Stephanie) house was built on sand was an understatement. Like Shelly, I had asked Jesus into my heart, but my actions didn't reflect the new life I had chosen. I was still running to other people and things on which to build my house. I had no firm foundation. I, too, had a failed marriage, was living paycheck to paycheck, had rocky relationships with my family, and unhealthy relationships with others.

I knew that I had to start living for Christ. I knew that I had to be a doer of the Word and make God my foundation. I went back to church and changed some behaviors, but it wasn't enough.

It wasn't until I began Bible study with Shelly that I truly began to understand how to apply the Word to my life and live like Jesus was asking of me. I am still a work in progress, I stumble quite a bit. But I am so much more content knowing that I have built my house on the foundation of Jesus and that, even if I do fall down, I have a Savior who will catch me. Abiding in Jesus has changed my entire life and has redirected my focus onto the Rock that will never let me down.

To continue in a particular attitude, condition, or relationship is the third definition of the word *abide*. This means that we will continue in our relationship with Christ, just like He continues in us. This means we don't "quit" God. We stay. We continue in Him through every experience and season of life. When we continue in God, we look to Him for guidance in the small things **and** the big things. We allow Him to affect every area of our life. We rely on Him to show us how to treat others and what paths we should take. We evaluate everything by asking, "Does this support he life He is trying to create for me?"

Relationships take work to continue in them. We will be talking about specific ways to abide later in this book.

Read the following verses. Write down your thoughts after reading each verse about abiding.

1. **1 John 3:24**—"Whoever keeps His commandments abides in God, and God in him. And by this we know that He abides in us, we know it by the Spirit whom He has given us."

_____

_____

_____

_____

Galatians 2:20—"I have been crucified with Christ. It is no longer I who live, but Christ who lives in me. And the life I now live in the flesh I live by faith in the Son of God, who loved me and gave Himself for me."

_____

_____

_____

_____

Lesson 2: How Do We Abide?

Section 1: Being Intentional

Okay. We know what you are probably thinking . . . "That's all fine and well, but just how am I supposed to do this . . . this abiding thing?"

The good news is, if you are completing this study, you are probably already abiding or on the right path to abiding! If you have confessed your sins and asked God into your heart, He is already abiding in you, and you are abiding in Him. The goal is to STAY there and rest there. John Piper says, "Hour-by-hour abiding in Jesus means hour-by-hour trusting Him to meet all your needs and be all our treasure." (2021). This means that we are continuously leaning into Him and relying on Him to guide us. We don't take a break, we don't turn to Him just when it's convenient, we are always in Christ's presence. This isn't always easy. I (Stephanie) struggle with this particularly when I'm at work. I find that I get so caught up in the immediate needs of my students, the pressing demands of phone calls and emails, and the busyness of the day that I end up shifting my focus from Christ's presence. I am working on making that change!

We need to become intentional about abiding in Christ, pursuing Him, and studying His Word. Abiding isn't something that just "happens." It takes purposeful dedication to walk with Jesus. Remember, God WANTS to be your dwelling place. John 14:23 (NIV) states, "Jesus replied, 'Anyone who loves me will obey my teaching. My Father will love them, and we will come to them and make our home with them.'"

You must make a conscious choice to walk with Him and to make His heart your home. Read 2 John 1:9, "Anyone who runs ahead and does not continue in the teaching of Christ does not have God; whoever continues in the teaching has both the Father and the Son."

What do you think Jesus means when He said "runs ahead and does not continue in the teaching of Christ . . ." in this verse?

_____

_____

_____

_____

As we said, abiding is deliberate. Consider the lives of Martha and Mary in Luke 10:38–42. If you aren't familiar with the story, let us set the stage for you. Jesus is visiting the home of the sisters and their brother, Lazarus. In verse 39, we find Mary sitting at Jesus' feet, steeping herself in all that Jesus has to say. She is intently focused on Him. Her sister, Mary, however, is in the kitchen taking care of all the things one has to tend to when you have company. As sisters often do, Martha gets irritated with Mary because she is not helping her complete the various tasks. And, as sisters often do, Martha decides to "tattle" on Mary to Jesus and begs Jesus to make Mary help her. She actually whines to Him about her sister. Verse 40: "She came to Him and asked, 'Lord, don't you care that my sister has left me to do the work by myself? Tell her to help me!'"

Note Jesus' response here. Luke 10:41–42, "But the Lord said to her, 'My dear Martha, you are worried and upset over all these details! There is only one thing worth being concerned about. Mary has discovered it, and it will not be taken away from her.'"

What do you think that Mary had discovered?

_____

_____

_____

_____

Mary had discovered the one thing that Jesus was talking about. She had discovered that to be in Jesus' presence is the most important way to spend her time. It is also the most important way for us to spend our time.

Section 2: Action Steps
So, how can we be more like Mary? It might seem unrealistic to take the time to just sit with Jesus with all the things we have to do these days. But allowing ourselves to become distracted by those things is exactly what Jesus was addressing. We have to **intentionally** carve out time to sit at His feet. Don't get stuck working in the kitchen when God is calling you to spend time with Him!

We can start by praying. This might seem like a simple act, but in fact, it is very important to our relationship with God. We know He wants us to pray to Him because there are many commands in the Bible that tell us to pray. Here is one of them. "Rejoice always, **pray without ceasing**, give thanks in all circumstances; for this is the will of God in Christ Jesus for you" (1 Thessalonians 5:16–18, emphasis added).

Some people can perceive prayer as an emergency line, like 91 They only turn to Jesus when there is a crisis in their life. Others perceive it as something they "should" do. They pray out of obligation from time to time, but their heart isn't fully into it. Still, others pray "on the go" or as they are falling asleep as an afterthought. The truth is that Jesus is our direct line to talk to God. *Prayer* is what connects us to God and enhances our relationship with Him. Jesus also wants us to pray to Him because that is the best way for Him to reveal Himself to us.

God is our Father and also our Best Friend. Consider for a moment how you communicate with your best friend. How often are you in contact with that person? How much time do you spend together? As you know, relationships take intentional actions to keep them healthy. The same is true of our relationship with Jesus. We need to talk with Him daily. Spend time with Him daily. We need to follow the same guidelines with Jesus as we would our best friend. Prayer serves this purpose and draws us closer to Him. It is important to CREATE time in your schedule to not only talk to God but to also wait and listen.

Does intentionally making time to spend with God seem realistic to you right now? Think about your daily schedule and try to find 10–15 minutes that you can set aside specifically for God. In what way could you rearrange your schedule to include intentional time for God?

_____

_____

_____

_____

Along with prayer, we also need to be studying His Word on a regular basis. By reading and studying the Word, we begin to understand the nature and character of our God and our covenant with Him. The more we dive into His Word, the more He reveals to us. The more He reveals to us, the more we come to truly know and love Him. The more we truly know and love Him, the closer we are to Him. Once you reach this point, spending time with God becomes a craving. #truth

Doing a Bible study like this one is a good place to start. We personally have found that it is difficult to just sit down with the Bible and try to start reading; although some people find this easy to do. We both need some sort of guidance to read along with the Bible so that we can gain more understanding about the passages and verses that we read. There are numerous Bible studies online, as well as commentaries that help explain the verses.

In a sermon on abiding, Mike Bickle suggests a strategy for reading the Bible. He calls it "pray-reading" the Word. He says that studying alone is not enough. It is important to talk with God while we study and to speak the Word back to Him. He says that "Bible study is meant to lead us to conversation with God by giving us the 'conversational material' for our prayer life" (Bickle, 2014).

He also lays out some steps that we can take while we are studying. First, we thank God for His truths. Second, we ask God to reveal His truths to us. We also commit to obeying God and ask God for the power to obey Him. By following these steps, Bible study becomes more meaningful, practical, and powerful. The more we dive into God's Word, the easier it becomes to understand the messages we are receiving from Him. Trust us when we tell you . . . when you ask for God to reveal something, He will reveal it to you! And sometimes that can be painful.

Having faith may not seem like an action step, but in reality, it is an important component of our intentional relationship with Jesus. Faith makes it possible for us to put our trust in God and STAY with Him, even when we don't feel Him. We will all have times in our lives when we might question where God is or what His will is for us, but faith helps us to abide during those difficult times.

We all know the story of Noah's Ark. Talk about FAITH! God was saddened by the hearts of the human race and decided to eliminate all life by flooding the earth. Noah, however, found favor with God and

He allowed Noah and his family to be spared. He gave Noah instructions on how to build an ark that would house his family and numerous pairs of animals throughout the flood. If we look at this from Noah's perspective, it would make sense that he may have had a few questions for God. If it were us, we sure would! It is speculated that the area where Noah lived had not ever seen rain or had not seen rain in a **very** long time. So, when God tells Noah that He is going to flood the earth, we're sure Noah was confused! Here God is asking him to build a massive ship and house the male and female of each animal on the earth while He sends enough rain to wipe out the rest of the population! Question number one . . . what is *rain*? Question number two . . . what is an *ark*? Question number three . . . why me?

Here is the passage found in Genesis 6:11–22.

> *"Now the earth was corrupt in God's sight and was full of violence. God saw how corrupt the earth had become, for all the people on earth had corrupted their ways. So God said to Noah, 'I am going to put an end to all people, for the earth is filled with violence because of them. I am surely going to destroy both them and the earth. So make yourself an ark of cypress wood; make rooms in it and coat it with pitch inside and out. This is how you are to build it: The ark is to be three hundred cubits long, fifty cubits wide, and thirty cubits high. Make a roof for it, leaving below the roof an opening one cubit high all around. Put a door in the side of the ark and make lower, middle, and upper decks. I am going to bring floodwaters on the earth to destroy all life under the heavens, every creature that has the breath of life in it. Everything on earth will perish. But I will establish my covenant with you, and you will enter the ark—you and your sons and your wife and your sons' wives with you.*

You are to bring into the ark two of all living crea-
tures, male and female, to keep them alive with you.
Two of every kind of bird, of every kind of animal, and
of every kind of creature that moves along the ground
will come to you to be kept alive. You are to take ev-
ery kind of food that is to be eaten and store it away
as food for you and for them.' Noah did everything
just as God commanded him."

Did you catch the last sentence of that passage? We'll share it
again. **"Noah did everything just as God commanded him"** (verse
22, emphasis added). The Bible doesn't mention one single incident
of Noah questioning or complaining. He just did as he was commanded! It took a huge amount of faith to simply say, "Yes, Lord."

Can we say that we do the same when God asks something of us?
Or do we demand to know the who, what, when, where, and why before we agree to do as we are asked? Do we have the kind of faith it
takes to follow through on God's commands? Can we faithfully say,
"Yes, Lord"? Likewise, do we have the kind of faith that is confident
that He is near even when we don't feel Him?

It is when we abide that we experience Him, and our faith is em-
boldened. Rest assured; He is always with us. Deuteronomy 31:8
(NIV) tells us, "The LORD Himself goes before you and will be with
you; He will never leave you nor forsake you. Do not be afraid; do not
be discouraged." He will NEVER leave you. Even when it seems like
you can't find or see Him, He is there with you. He is walking beside
you, holding your hand. He is there, helping us do the things He asks
of us. However, when we abide, it is easier to be aware of His presence during trials in our life.

Has there been a time in your life when you felt your faith was weak?

_____

_____

_____

_____

Has there been a time in your life where your faith held you up during a difficult time?

_____

_____

_____

_____

Section 3: But Wait, There's More!

Giving thanks is another intentional step we can take to help us abide in Christ. When we take time to stop and think about the blessings God has poured upon us and thank Him for them, we draw nearer to Him.

You have most likely received a thoughtful gift from someone. When you received the gift that was hand-picked just for you with you in their mind, you probably felt loved and appreciated by that person. You were probably thankful and filled with feelings of joy. You probably felt closer to that person as you expressed your gratitude.

This is what happens when we tell Jesus how much we appreciate all He has done for and given to us. We are filled with feelings of joy and we feel closer to Him as we express our gratitude.

Read Colossians 2:6–7, "So then, just as you received Christ Jesus as Lord, continue to live your lives **in** Him, rooted and built up **in** Him, strengthened in the faith as you were taught, and **overflowing with thankfulness**" (emphasis added).

Some days, it can be harder to find something to be grateful for than others. If we end up focusing on all the things that are going wrong in our lives, we tend to lose focus on Jesus. It is extremely easy to fall into this trap. When we focus on the negative, eventually it becomes all that we see. It becomes harder to find things to be grateful for. When we are feeling like God is allowing bad things to happen, the human side of us does not want to show gratitude. In 1 Thessalonians 5:18, we are instructed to "give thanks in all circumstances; for this is God's will for you in Christ Jesus." That doesn't mean to thank him FOR your circumstances. It says to give thanks IN all circumstances. Those are two completely different prepositions! Never forget that he is WITH you through everything, which gives us a compelling reason to be thankful.

It is important for us to remember that we are only here for a little while and we will only have troubles for that short time. Look at what 2 Corinthians 4:17 says, "For our light and momentary troubles are achieving for us an eternal glory that far outweighs them all." Did you notice that Paul (the writer of 2 Corinthians) labeled our troubles as **light and momentary**? What he means is that even though our issues here might seem devastating, they are very small in comparison to what lies ahead for us in Heaven. The greatness of what God has to offer us outshines our difficulties here on Earth. When we focus on spending eternity with God, our current troubles don't seem quite as catastrophic.

When we turn our attention to the blessings in our lives, it helps us to stay centered on Jesus. Even on our worst days, we can be thankful that Jesus loves us so much that He sacrificed Himself for us. In Romans 5:8 (NIV) we read, "But God demonstrates His own love for us in this: While we were still sinners, Christ died for us."

This means that before we were born, Christ had us on His mind as He was dying on the cross. You, friend. He did that for you. That is definitely something to be grateful for. So, if there is nothing else that you are thankful for in this big beautiful world, be thankful that Jesus died and rose again to wipe out your sins and to redeem you!

Take a moment and list at least five things that you are thankful for in your life. Save it . . . come back to this list on those days when you are feeling less than thankful. And keep adding to this list as a reminder of the wonderful things God has placed in your life!

_____

_____

_____

_____

_____

The last action step that we are going to talk about is one of our favorites. Praise and worship! We cannot express how much we absolutely love rejoicing and worshipping!

There has been an abundance of times where we have been worshipping with song, and we begin crying (okay, maybe every time). Both of us have had experiences of being overwhelmed by the Spirit during worship times. There is something about worship that allows for complete vulnerability before the Spirit. If you have experienced this, you know exactly what we are talking about! Don't get us wrong, there are other things that do that too, like prayer and Bible study. For us, *worship* is a tool that allows us to bare our hearts and allows for absolute surrender. Talk about feeling close to Him! To be honest, words can't really describe it, but we'll try.

When we worship and rejoice in Him, we are able to concentrate solely on Him and how much He loves us. We do our best to shut out the outside world (including those standing around us) and just bask in His presence. We open ourselves up to the Spirit and allow Him to shine through us. It is one of the most beautiful experiences one can have.

There is an unspeakable joy as described in 1 Peter 1:8 (NIV), "Though you have not seen Him, you love Him; and even though you do not see Him now, you believe in Him and are filled with an inexpressible and glorious joy." Although the verse states that joy is "inexpressible," we often find that we express that joy through tears.

The most important reason praise and worship are essential is that they bring pleasure to God. Above all else, He is more than worthy of our praise! Revelation 4:11 says, "Our Lord and God, You are worthy to receive glory and honor and power, because You have created all things, and by Your will they exist and were created." We exist because He created us! We have life because He continues to give us life. We have wonderful things and people in our lives because He gives them to us. He carries us through difficult times. Praise the Lord! Psalm 29:2 tells us to "Give unto the Lord the glory due into His name; worship the Lord in the beauty of holiness" (KJV).

Amazing things happen when we praise the Lord! Do you know the story of Jehoshaphat and his army going to battle against a seemingly undefeatable army? When Jehoshaphat and his army went to battle, he made the surprising decision to send ahead "appointed men to sing to the Lord and to praise Him for the splendor of His holiness as they went out at the head of the army, saying: 'Give thanks to the Lord, for His love endures forever'" (2 Chronicles 20:21). He sent singers ahead of the army! From a military standpoint, that doesn't make a lot of sense. Wouldn't he want to send his strongest and most fierce warriors first? Nope. He sent the choir! Jehoshaphat knew the power of worship!

WHAT HAPPENED? Well, as the story unfolds, because of Jehoshaphat's praise, the Lord caused the armies that were coming against Jehoshaphat to turn from their pursuit of him and begin fighting one another. The opposing army was completely destroyed, and Jehoshaphat's army was victorious. Wow! Think about the evil we can defeat with our praise. Our enemy, the devil, is a real and manipulative foe. But he cannot be in any place where there are sincere shouts and songs of praise. He cannot remain there. Does the devil have you feeling down, defeated, or just grumpy in general? Dig deep in your heart and sing sincere songs of praise to Jesus. The devil will HAVE to flee. Psalm 66:1–3 reads, "'Shout for joy to God, all the earth! Sing the glory of His name; make His praise glorious. Say to God, 'How awesome are Your deeds! So great is Your power that Your enemies cringe before You.'" Praise gives us a direct pathway to tap into God's strength. Praise allows us to feel God's power.

Did you know that the act of worship actually modifies the chemistry in our brains? It's scientific, yet supernatural. Positive thoughts bring positive outcomes. "Forming a habit of worship changes our brain structure and our thought-life gets overwritten with the truth of the goodness of God." (Beliefnet, 2016). Praise and worship will reshape the framework of our brains and alter the way we think. Instead of making the world the spotlight of our thoughts, Jesus takes over that spotlight and becomes our focal point. Worshipping renews our minds.

Stop right here and find your favorite worship tunes. You can write them down here if you'd like. Spend 5 minutes (or longer) offering sincere praise to our Heavenly Father, for He is good!

_____

_____

_____

_____

Section 4: Attaching to the Vine

To explain the concept of attaching to the Vine, let's start by visualizing an actual vine. A grapevine has a vine and branches, and the grapes grow on the branches of the plant. If the branches are not attached to the vine, they will fall to the ground and wither because the vine is no longer supplying the branch with life. Any fruit they have produced will die also. Once the branch has been detached from the vine, it can no longer produce fruit or live.

Why did we choose to talk about the grapevine? Because our relationship with Jesus operates in the same manner.

Let's take a moment to think about the definition of *abide*. If you recall, the first definition of *abide* means to "remain; continue; stay." Keep that definition in mind as you read the following verse.

"Remain in Me, as I also remain in you. No branch can bear fruit by itself; it must remain in the vine. Neither can you bear fruit unless you remain in Me" (John 15:4). Jesus is telling us to remain **in** Him. He is telling us that we cannot bear any fruit unless we are connected to Him. Being connected to Jesus is essential in your walk with Christ.

When we abide in Jesus, we become attached to the Vine (Jesus). We become the branches that bear His fruit. He makes it clear that we cannot bear His fruit unless we are attached to Him. If we are not attached to Him, our lifeline is cut off. We are not talking about immediate physical death, but a spiritual death in which we would be separated from Christ for eternity.

Attaching ourselves to the Vine and abiding in Him is fundamental for life and our spiritual growth. We must trust that we get all we need from the Vine.

Read John 15:5, "I am the Vine; you are the branches. If you remain in Me and I in you, you will bear much fruit; apart from Me you can do nothing."

Why do you think Jesus said we can do nothing apart from Him?

_____

_____

_____

_____

John 15:1–2 says, "I am the true vine, and my Father is the gardener. He cuts off every branch in Me that bears no fruit, while every branch that does bear fruit, He prunes so that it will be even more fruitful." In this parable, Jesus is teaching us that we are the branches that connect to Him, and He is the vine. Jesus also talks about His Father being the gardener or vinedresser. A gardener prunes his plants so that they will produce the best and most fruit. Without pruning, plants will grow extra parts that will take the nutrition away from the fruit, thus damaging the fruit. Gardeners often refer to those extra parts as *suckers*. The gardener will cut off those extra parts so that the fruit will receive all the nutrition it needs.

God is our Gardener.

Think about what this process might look like in your life. Pruning can sometimes be painful, yet necessary. Those suckers must be removed! This could be a relationship ending; the loss of material things, habits, or beliefs; the end or change of a career; or, even the ending of dreams. Sometimes these can be what we perceive as good things, but if they cause us to stop growing or focusing on Him, God will prune them from our lives. We need to ask for God's wisdom to understand and accept when pruning takes place.

What possible suckers does God need to prune from your life so that you can receive all that you need and stay focused on Him? How would you respond if you thought those suckers were important to you?

_____

_____

_____

_____

Take a few minutes and read the entire chapter of John 15 (don't worry, it's short). Use the following space to jot down which verses stand out to you. Make a note about how remaining connected to Jesus affects your spiritual growth.

_____

_____

_____

_____

Lesson 3: What Happens When We Abide?

So many good things happen when we abide! Doesn't it feel great to steep yourself in God's word and God's love? When we abide, we develop a close, personal relationship with God.

As we covered in the last section, Jesus described himself as the Vine and His Father as the Vinedresser. God is the great Gardener, providing sustenance to us, His disciples. He provides all the spiritual nutrition we need for growth, and He prunes out the life-sucking weeds that are meant to destroy us.

If we were to delve into all the blessings that we receive when we abide, this book would be way too long. So instead, we are going to focus on just a few of the blessings that come with abiding.

One blessing that we experience when we abide is that of answered prayers. Don't misunderstand here . . . we are not talking about a magical formula that grants you whatever you wish. Let's read John 15:7, "If you remain in Me and My words remain in you, ask whatever you wish, and it will be done for you." Notice that Jesus doesn't say "Ask for anything and I'll give it to you." He says that if we remain in Him and His words remain in us, THEN we can ask for what we want.

What this means is that when we abide, our hearts become more aligned with Jesus' heart. We start wanting what Jesus wants and our prayers become more in line with His will. We are able to hear His voice more clearly which in turn leads to more powerful prayers. Abiding provides us with a TRUE UNION with Christ.

Take a moment to write down a prayer request.

_____

_____

_____

_____

Now ask God to reveal His heart in your prayer. Does your prayer line up with the will of God?

God will always answer our prayers. His answer will arrive in one of three ways. He will either say *yes, no,* or *wait.* Sometimes, our prayers aren't answered to our liking, which can leave us angry or disappointed with God. When we receive an answer of no, we sometimes feel that God has let us down. However, that isn't the case! God gives us what we NEED. Not always what we WANT. Sometimes what we want might cause harm to ourselves or someone else even though we may not realize it. Keep in mind, HE knows what the future holds, and He knows what's best for us. Romans 8:28 reads, "And we know that all things work together for good to those who love God, to those who are called according to His purpose." We will go through both positive and negative experiences during our lifetime. The assurance that Romans 8:28 is giving us is that we know God will use all those things (both positive and negative) for the good of His kingdom, which will create blessings for us. We need to trust Him that He will give us exactly what we need.

In John 15:15, we discover another blessing of abiding in Christ. "I no longer call you servants, because a servant does not know His master's business. Instead, I have called you friends, for everything that I learned from My Father I have made known to you."

Did you hear what He is saying in that passage? He calls us FRIENDS! The Son of God, High King, and Creator of everything calls you "His friend." He took us from slavery and promoted us to one of His inner circles. That is a really **big deal**! Historically speaking, friendship had a different connotation than it does today. In Jesus' day, friendship was a very important relationship in society. There was a presumption that one would lay down his life for a friend (O'Day, 2008). We don't often think about whether or not we would die for a friend. Typically, we toss around the word *friend* to even include a casual acquaintance, but we don't comprehend the true meaning of that word as it was used by Jesus.

When Jesus stated that He calls us His friends, that's exactly what He means. In John 15:13, we read, "Greater love has no one than this: to lay down one's life for one's friends." This is the type of friendship that they experienced during those times.

Isn't that what Jesus did for us?? YES! He willingly laid down His life for us. For me. For you. That is a profound and unfathomable friendship! So many people, including followers of Christ, don't understand this level of friendship. But in order to comprehend the depths of Jesus' love for us, it is important that we don't miss the significance that was placed on the relationship called friendship.

How does it make you feel knowing that Jesus says that He is your friend and that He died for you? How can you ensure that you are offering the same level of friendship to Jesus?

_____

_____

_____

_____

Reflect on chapter one of John. What was your biggest takeaway? Did you see something in a new light? What do you think your next steps will be?

_____

_____

_____

_____

CHAPTER 2

FRUIT OF THE SPIRIT

One of the biggest blessings of abiding in Christ is that we produce His fruit. There are a total of nine fruits that are listed in Galatians 5:22–23. "But the fruit of the Spirit is love, joy, peace, patience, kindness, goodness, faithfulness, gentleness, and self-control. Against such things there is no law."

We will be looking at each one of these individually because while it is so exciting to bear fruit for Jesus, we are unable to produce this fruit unless we **abide**.

Take a moment to recall the first time you heard anything about the fruit of the Spirit. Where were you? What was your impression?

_____

_____

_____

_____

Lesson 1: What Is the Fruit of the Spirit?

Fruit of the Spirit is something children learn about in Sunday school in every church ever built. So, for those who grew up in church, you probably feel very familiar with these characteristics. Some of you have learned about them as adults. Still others of you may not know what they are at all. Whatever your knowledge level is about them, we are hopeful that you will be able to apply the concepts in this study to your life.

At first glance, this could appear as a list of behaviors that God expects from Christians. If you were to skip the rest of chapter 5 in Galatians and just read those two verses, they could definitely come across as expectations and are often taught as such. We can try to live out these characteristics without abiding, but we will fail miserably. We will always feel like we are not doing enough. We will find ourselves saying, "I need to work harder at loving people." Or, "I need to pray for patience." Or, "I need to find peace in this situation." The harsh reality is that no matter how hard we try, we cannot accomplish these things on our own. We cannot love everyone. We cannot maintain self-control or patience in every situation. We cannot even find joy half the time. Those children of ours are going to push our buttons. Our spouses are going to leave their dirty socks on the rug. Someone at work is going to cause us to feel less than kind and loving as we should. This "list of expectations" is not humanly possible. No matter how hard we try, we will fail. The *fruit of the Spirit* is a set of characteristics that we are able to demonstrate once we have started following Jesus. Sure, we can exhibit some of them to an extent, but the true potential of the fruit isn't realized without the help of the Holy Spirit.

It wasn't until recently that we realized that looking at the fruits as a list of expectations was skewed thinking. It is true that God expects us to live out the fruit of the Spirit, but the good news is that WE do not have to grow the fruit on our own. What a relief! The *fruit of the Spirit* is essentially God's character. God is love. God is joy. God is peace, etc. You can plug in any of the nine fruits and God is all those things, right?

Many beautiful things happen when we accept the gift of salvation. One of the best is that we allow God to abide in us, which means that His FRUIT also abides in us. His character becomes our character. And the closer we get to God, the more fruit He produces within us. Look at John 15:5 again. "I am the vine; you are the branches. If you remain in Me and I in you, you will bear much fruit; **apart from me you can do nothing**" (emphasis added). He says it right there, **we cannot do it on our own**.

Remember that grapevine we told you about? If we are going to bear fruit—authentic fruit—we must remain connected to the Vine. When we do, HIS fruit naturally becomes our fruit. If we try to live in our own strength, we will not produce HIS fruit. The stronger our relationship with God, the more we love others, the more patience we demonstrate, the more joy we feel, etc. It's not human strength. It is His supernatural strength.

This is our ultimate purpose while we are here on Earth. God has designed us to produce His fruit and bring others to a relationship with Him. In Colossians, Paul tells us this very fact. Colossians 1:10–12, "so that you may live a life worthy of the Lord and please Him in every way: bearing fruit in every good work, growing in the knowledge of God, being strengthened with all power according to His glorious might so that you may have great endurance and patience, and giving joyful thanks to the Father, who has qualified you to share in the inheritance of His holy people in the kingdom of light." This is why we felt led to write this study.

Instead of reading the entire book of Galatians right now (although reading it isn't a bad idea, and we suggest doing so), we will try to sum up what Paul meant when he was talking about the fruit.

Paul was trying to clarify the truth of salvation by sharing the importance of grace over law. The Galatians knew the truth but had been listening to false teachings that emphasized salvation through works and rules. They were beginning to believe that they could "earn" their way into Heaven by their actions. In Galatians 2:21, Paul states, "I do not set aside the grace of God, for if righteousness could be gained through the law, then Christ died for nothing!" He is basically saying, what was the point of the cross if we have to follow the laws to get into Heaven?

Let's fast forward to Galatians 5 to better understand Paul's statement about the fruit of the Spirit. Starting in verse 13 through verse 21:

> *"You, my brothers and sisters, were called to be free. But do not use your freedom to indulge the flesh; rather, serve one another humbly in love. For the entire law is fulfilled in keeping this one command: Love your neighbor as yourself. If you bite and devour each other, watch out or you will be destroyed by each other. So I say,* **walk by the Spirit, and you will not gratify the desires of the flesh**. *For the flesh desires what is contrary to the Spirit, and the Spirit what is contrary to the flesh. They are in conflict with each other, so that you are not to do whatever you want. But if you are led by the Spirit, you are not under the law. The acts of the flesh are obvious: sexual immorality, impurity, and debauchery; idolatry and witchcraft; hatred, discord, jealousy, fits of rage, selfish ambition, dissensions, factions and envy; drunkenness, orgies, and the like. I warn you, as I did before, that those who live like this will not inherit the kingdom of God" (emphasis added).*

What is Paul saying here? He is telling us that if we are walking in the Spirit, we will not want to be walking in the flesh and doing those naughty things because they are opposed to one another, and the Spirit will resist the flesh. Sounds simple, right? Walk with Jesus, bear perfect fruit, avoid bad fruit, live happily ever after. We all want that! So why is it so difficult for Christians to resist the desires of the flesh? The short answer: Because we are human. We have a natural capacity to sin. When we are lacking fellowship (abiding) with God, we are more likely to sin. There is a constant battle within us and, ultimately, it is our decision to walk in the Spirit or walk in the flesh. It is so much easier to walk in the Spirit when we are abiding. What we focus on determines our fruit.

When we seek an intimate relationship with our Father, the fruit freely grows. When you are close to God, you will be overflowing with fruit, and you will freely give that fruit to others. Be deliberate about deepening your relationship with God and let Him shape you. Allow HIS fruit to grow. John 15:8 reads, "This is to my Father's glory, that you bear much fruit, showing yourselves to be My disciples."

Anyone can look at a plant and tell if it is healthy or not. A healthy plant is attached to a vine, is green, and is producing fruit. If it is unhealthy, it is usually brown and has no fruit attached. Be cautious about what vine your branch is attached to. It is too easy to become attached to earthly things (money, the Internet, work, sports, television, video games, alcohol, drugs, shopping, sex, etc.) so we need to stay vigilant.

What vine are you currently attached to? What kind of fruit are you producing?

_____

_____

_____

_____

By the fruit that you are bearing, what can people tell about your relationship with God?

_____

_____

_____

_____

Galatians 6:7–8 says, "Do not be deceived: God cannot be mocked. A man reaps what he sows. Whoever sows to please their flesh, from the flesh will reap destruction; whoever sows to please the Spirit, from the Spirit will reap eternal life."

Instead of becoming attached to an earthly vine, make the pursuit of God your priority. Make sure that you are attached to the Vine of life. Matthew 6:33 says, "But seek first His kingdom and His righteousness, and all these things will be given to you as well."

Now we will be diving into the individual fruits. They can be viewed in three groups of three. The first three, love, joy, and peace, are fruits that focus on God. The next three, patience, kindness, and goodness, focus on others. The final three, faithfulness, gentleness, and self-control, focus on ourselves.

Lesson 2: Love

The first fruit of the Spirit is _love_. It is no mistake that Paul listed love first. After all, isn't God love over all other things? God doesn't just show or demonstrate love to us, He IS love. His entire being is love. That is why when the disciples asked Jesus what the greatest commandment in the law was, "Jesus replied: 'Love the Lord your God with all your heart and with all your soul and with all your mind.'

This is the first and greatest commandment. And the second is like it: 'Love your neighbor as yourself.' All the Law and the Prophets hang on these two commandments" (Matthew 22:37–40).

We use the word *love* so freely and frivolously in our society. For example, I *love* these potato chips; I *love* this song; I *love* that shirt! However, *love* is not just a warm feeling towards something or someone. It is a deliberate and purposeful attitude. Love allows us to give freely, whether the other person deserves it or not, and without expecting anything in return.

This type of love is a special kind of love. In the Greek language, it even has its own translation, setting it apart from other types of love by naming them differently. Some of the words for love in Greek include *eros*, which is a passionate and physical type of love; *storge* (pronounced *store-gay*), which is a love for family; and, *philia*, which is a brotherly and friendly type of love. The spiritual fruit of love we are referring to here is called *agape*, which is a perfect love from God. *Agape love* is the "highest level of love referenced in the Bible. This form of love is everlasting and sacrificial, whether or not the giver receives the same level of love in return" (Smyth, 2020).

Agape love is described for us in 1 Corinthians 13:4–8, "Love is patient, love is kind. It does not envy, it does not boast, it is not proud. It does not dishonor others, it is not self-seeking, it is not easily angered, it keeps no record of wrongs. Love does not delight in evil but rejoices with the truth. It always protects, always trusts, always hopes, always perseveres. Love never fails . . . ."

We cannot express agape love without the power of the Holy Spirit. Human love on its own often comes with conditions. God's love, agape love, has no conditions. He loves us as we are, and we are to show this love to others. No exceptions.

Depending on the version of the Bible you read, you will read the word *love* no less than 310 times. Some versions have this word more than 500 times! The point being made here (and in the Bible) is that love is the central concept on which everything else is built. Circling back to the book of John, let's read John 15:17. "This is My command: Love each other."

Read John 15:17 again. "This is My command: Love each other." This is not a gentle, "Hey, if you don't mind, could you love on some people for me?" or an "If you get around to it" kind of commandment. We are even called to love our enemies. Most of us would say that we don't have enemies, per se, but really think about it. Is there someone you don't really get along with? Someone who grates on your nerves a little too much? Someone who has hurt or is currently trying to hurt you? Jesus would define those as *enemies*. Matthew 5:44 says, "But I tell you, love your enemies and pray for those who persecute you." What a challenging request!

Also, we can perform all kinds of good deeds, do all kinds of things for the church, help the needy, etc., but, **if we don't have love none of it matters**! Read 1 Corinthians 13:1–3:

> *"If I speak in the tongues of men or of angels, but do not have love, **I am only a resounding gong or a clanging cymbal**. If I have the gift of prophecy and can fathom all mysteries and all knowledge, and if I have a faith that can move mountains, but do not have love, **I am nothing**. If I give all I possess to the poor and give over my body to hardship that I may boast, but do not have love, **I gain nothing**" (emphasis added).*

Is it difficult for you to follow Christ's example of love, showing love to ALL? Why or why not?

_____

_____

_____

_____

As you spend more time abiding in Christ, how can you be more purposeful in outwardly expressing agape love toward others?

_____

_____

_____

_____

Lesson 3: Joy

The second fruit of the Spirit is *joy*. Dictionary.com defines *joy* as "the emotion of great delight or happiness caused by something exceptionally good or satisfying" (2021). Every time I (Shelly) hear the word *joy*, I instinctively start to sing the old song of my youth, "I've got the joy, joy, joy, joy down in my heart." Unfortunately, the world seems to be short on joy these days, wouldn't you agree?

What gives you joy?

_____

_____

_____

What did you list that gives you joy? Family? Friends? Coffee? Shopping? Chocolate? While these things are all wonderful and satisfying, they cannot provide us with authentic, unshakable joy. Let us explain.

The definition above describes *joy* as an emotion. Whereas the joy that Jesus brings is a state of mind and not a fickle feeling. Jesus gives a lasting and steadfast joy that is dependent upon His love and promises that never change. The world offers things that can bring us joy, but this type of joy is fleeting and limited. It would actually be considered temporary happiness as opposed to true joy. Worldly happiness is based upon things like whether life events go well, whether someone likes us, or whether we are successful, etc. As soon as our circumstances change, that feeling of happiness goes away. That type of joy will never last. Worldly joy is #fakenews!

The joy that Jesus gives is based upon the promise that if we believe in Him, we are accepted into His eternal family. No matter what happens in our life, NOTHING can take that away from us. Romans 8:38–39 reminds us that "neither death nor life, neither angels nor demons, neither the present nor the future, nor any powers, neither height nor depth, nor anything else in all creation, will be able to separate us from the love of God that is in Christ Jesus our Lord."

Paul lived his life based on this promise. He knew the joy that comes from having a relationship with Jesus. He endured numerous trials and hardships after becoming a disciple of Christ. His life of sharing the Gospel was not easy! Read what he writes in 2 Corinthians 11:24–28.

"Five times I received from the Jews the forty lashes minus one. Three times I was beaten with rods, once I was pelted with stones, three times I was shipwrecked, I spent a night and a day in the open sea, I have been constantly on the move. I have been in danger from

rivers, in danger from bandits, in danger from my fellow Jews, in danger from Gentiles; in danger in the city, in danger in the country, in danger at sea; and in danger from false believers. I have labored and toiled and have often gone without sleep; I have known hunger and thirst and have often gone without food; I have been cold and naked. Besides everything else, I face daily the pressure of my concern for all the churches."

Wow! Paul certainly had a lot of reasons to be stressed and distraught!

But if you read any of the books of the Bible that he wrote, you will not hear him complaining. On the contrary, he talks continuously about persevering and having the type of joy that is based upon Jesus. He talks about how he has been able to be content no matter what. In Philippians 4:11–13, he writes, "I am not saying this because I am in need, for I have learned to be content whatever the circumstances. I know what it is to be in need, and I know what it is to have plenty. I have learned the secret of being content in any and every situation, whether well fed or hungry, whether living in plenty or in want. I can do all this through Him who gives me strength." That is an unshakable joy!

The Greek word for joy is *chara*, which refers to a "feeling of inner gladness, delight, or rejoicing. It is a depth of assurance and confidence that ignites a cheerful heart—and in turn, that cheerful heart leads to cheerful behavior" (Seale, 2018). This is the type of joy that Paul was talking about and James was referring to in the book of James.

In James 1:2–4 he writes, "Consider it pure joy, my brothers and sisters, whenever you face trials of many kinds, because you know that the testing of your faith produces perseverance. Let perseverance finish its work so that you may be mature and complete, not lacking anything."

When I (Stephanie) read this verse for the first time, I thought James was crazy. Consider it pure joy when I face troubles? That was a hard concept for me to grasp. How can I consider things like relationship troubles something to be joyful about? Even after the death of my daughter, I wondered what part of it I was to consider joyful. The more I grow with Christ, however, I am starting to understand what James meant. I do not have to be joyful about upsetting circumstances, but I can hold onto the joy that Christ gives me during those times. No matter what happens around me, I know that there is nothing that can take away my relationship with Christ and that alone gives me joy.

Wouldn't it be wonderful to have the foundation of joy that both Paul and James talked about; the joy that comes with the confidence that ignites a cheerful heart in all circumstances? You can! Jesus offers the same gift to us. When we consider all that Christ has done for us, it is hard to not be joyful. Christ was born into a sinful world to ultimately die a horrific death. Then, He was resurrected so that we can become reconciled to God and be with God for eternity. Not only did He suffer for us, but He also did this willingly! That joy isn't based upon a bad day at work, or car problems, or how many mistakes you make. That joy is based upon His love for us that never fades!

Jesus tells us in John 15:11 that "I have told you this so that My joy may be in you and that your joy may be complete." **Complete**. Not partial. Not lacking anything. Not based on the conditions of the world. But **complete**. No other joy that the world provides can be nearly as complete as the joy Jesus gives.

Think about a moment in which your happiness was ruined because of the circumstances of the day. How can having complete joy in Jesus help your mood and attitude when things go "wrong"?

_____

_____

_____

_____

How much joy fills your heart when you think of what He went through for you, knowing how much He loves you?

_____

_____

_____

_____

Lesson 4: Peace

Do you long for peace? A lot of us do. We desperately wish for an hour of quietness. We hide in the bathroom for a few minutes to escape the noise. We hit snooze a couple of times for a little more sleep. We pray for harmonious relationships with family, friends, coworkers, or with the world. We tell each other that we just wish we had some peace in our lives.

Surprisingly, the word *peace* takes on several different meanings in the Bible. It is not just the absence of chaos or conflict. It is not just about having a calm center amid strife. If you stop there, you are missing the mark. We know we did at first. As a matter of fact, we rewrote this whole lesson based on a new understanding.

Part of biblical peace requires knowing that the Lord is close and resting on the assurance that He will never leave us. It means not allowing any circumstance to steal the inner peace that we obtain from Jesus.

In his letter to the Philippians, Paul talks about this kind of peace. "And the peace of God, which transcends all understanding, will guard your hearts and your minds in Christ Jesus" (Philippians 4:7). Paul is saying that this *peace*, the peace of God, is present in the midst of everything we might experience. He means that amidst the small, annoying troubles (like that driver going too slowly on the highway) or catastrophic problems (like a loved one dying too soon), we can still have the peace of God.

In the book of Mark (chapter 4, verses 35–39), the disciples were not abiding in Jesus even though they were with Him in a ship, and they allowed their peace to be stolen from them. A violent storm arose, and waves pelted the boat. The disciples were panicking, but Jesus was sleeping. They woke Him up begging Him to save them.

Let's pause here for a minute. Our life is often like that storm that arose on the disciples. Ours is a figurative storm, not an actual one, but it's very turbulent just the same. The waves that pelt our boat are financial issues, relationship troubles, work stress, health concerns, and so much more. Are you panicking as the disciples did? Are you begging God to save you from your troubles? We want you to see how Jesus responded to them at that moment.

Reading Mark 4:39 (KJV), "And He arose, and rebuked the wind, and said unto the sea, 'Peace, be still.' And the wind ceased, and there was a great calm."

Instead of begging Jesus to take away our problems, we can simply ask Him to calm our hearts. Ask Him to tell our hearts, "Peace, be still." That is the peace that transcends understanding. A peace that anchors our hearts even though things around us seem to be crumbling. It is a peace that rests on the truth that God is in control, and we can trust in Him to care for us; thus giving us peace despite the storm.

This is hard for our human brains to understand. This is why Paul dubbed this peace the kind that "transcends all understanding." We so easily allow circumstances to steal our peace. But the peace that can be snatched away by our environment is not peace from God. God's peace is not the absence of noise and chaos, but a tranquil feeling even when the world around you is falling apart. It is an internal calm, knowing that God is in control. This peace can only be obtained by abiding.

Are you easily frazzled by situations surrounding your life? Think of a specific time you felt overwhelmed by the waves of the storm. Were you able to remember that God was in control and surrender to His peace? Write down your reflections.

Ask God right now to fill your heart with His supernatural peace. Ask Him to help you to anchor your heart to Him no matter what is happening in your life. Write out that prayer here.

_____

_____

_____

_____

There is another part of biblical peace that we are certain is not discussed in Sunday school class. As we were researching and writing, we were hit with new knowledge like a freight train, "God's holy freight train."

We often associate the word *peace* with the absence of conflict. While this can be a true statement, biblical peace also involves diving into and engaging with conflict instead of running away from it. Don't mistake that statement as a reason to fight, but more as a call for unity. It is impossible to have complete peace and unity without facing and restoring what has been destroyed. There are many times in the Bible where we are called to reconciliation and to live in peace. 2 Corinthians 13:11, "Finally, brothers and sisters, rejoice! **Strive for full restoration, encourage one another, be of one mind, live in peace**. And the God of love and peace will be with you" (emphasis added).

We also are told in James 3:18 that "Peacemakers who sow in peace reap a harvest of righteousness." We know that we will reap what we sow, and if we strive to seek peace and resolve conflict, we will reap righteousness. Psalm 34:14 tells us to "turn from evil and do good; seek peace and pursue it." That makes it pretty clear; we are to work toward promoting biblical peace, both within our own lives and the lives of those around us.

Romans 12:18 says, "If it is possible, as far as it depends on you, live at peace with everyone." Is there a conflict in your life that needs reconciliation?

Meditate on this verse and ask God to reveal to you what it is He would have you do to pursue peace.

Lesson 5: Patience

First, we need to explain that this patience is not necessarily what we typically perceive patience to be. To be honest, this revelation did not hit us until we started writing this section. And, once again, it hit like a freight train. We prayed for God's wisdom and guidance, and He delivered it on that train.

We thought that we would be writing about how to have patience while waiting on something. You know, to have patience while stuck in traffic, to have patience while waiting for payday, to have patience while waiting for the doctor to call back, and to have patience with our screaming children, etc. And while the Biblical meaning of *patience* does include all of that, there is so much more.

In the Bible, the word *patience* is synonymous with "long-suffering, lenience, perseverance, steadfastness, and forbearance." We could see how words like *perseverance* and *steadfastness* would be synonyms for *patience*, but what about *long-suffering, lenience,* and *forbearance*? We accepted that they were of the same meaning, but we really didn't understand the connection. Until . . . Until we started researching. Until we learned what God truly means about being patient.

The word used in Galatians 5:22 for patience literally means "long-suffering." The word *long-suffering* is made up of two Greek words that mean "long" and "temper" (Compelling Truth, 2021). So, this is where we get the "long temper" definition of *patience*. When we demonstrate long-suffering, we are slow to anger. We have the ability to hold back our temper for a long time. We read in James 1:19–20, "My dear brothers and sisters, take note of this: Everyone should be quick to listen, slow to speak, and slow to become angry because human anger does not produce the righteousness that God desires."

When God asks us to be patient, He is asking us to persevere and endure **without striking back** when life and others treat us badly. Proverbs 19:11 states "A person's wisdom yields patience: it is to one's glory to overlook offense." We are supposed to tolerate ill-treatment from others, without getting mad at them and flying off the handle. Simply put, we are to respond to trials and frustrating situations with love.

Don't get us wrong, this doesn't mean that we do not feel anger. This does not mean that we do not ever get upset. What this means is that even though we might feel angry or hurt, we neither lash out at others from those emotions nor do we remain angry. Ephesians 4:26–27 tells us, "In your anger do not sin: Do not let the sun go down while you are still angry, and do not give the devil a foothold." We can acknowledge our emotions and allow ourselves to feel them, but we do not base our reactions on them. We also do not allow ourselves to stay stuck in our anger or frustration.

Ephesians 4:3 says, "Make every effort to keep the unity of the Spirit through the bond of peace." This means that we are to remain calm and patient when we are dealing with life's problems. We are to smile at those who cut us off on the highway. We are to show loving kindness when we experience someone who is unkind or unfair.

Sounds difficult? It is! We do not have the power to exhibit this kind of patience on our own! Once again, we can only succeed in this endeavor with the help of the Holy Spirit! This, then, is where abiding comes in. When we abide in Christ, He endows us with the ability to express the kind of patience He desires for us. Think about the patience God has with us. How many times do we fail? How often do we sin? How often would a human reach a frustration level with us when God shows complete mercy and forgiveness? He is showing us how we should behave.

The more time you spend abiding in Christ, the better you will be able to respond like Christ would when that person cuts you off in traffic, when the fast food place gets your order wrong, when someone is dishonest with you, or when life is just generally unfair. And isn't that our goal? To become more like Christ?

Stop here for a few moments and ponder this verse: "Do not be quickly provoked in your spirit, for anger resides in the lap of fools" (Ecclesiastes 7:9). What is being said here? Does this verse apply to your life in any way?

_____

_____

_____

_____

Are you easily provoked by life's irritants or are you able to tap into the Holy Spirit when faced with adversity? Why do you think you respond as you do?

_____

_____

_____

_____

If you are like us and need help remaining patient when you are dealing with life's struggles, we suggest praying and asking God to help you. As you abide in Christ, here is a suggested verse for you to pray daily.

> *"Lord, be gracious to us; we long for You. Be our strength every morning, our salvation in time of distress" (Isaiah 33:2).*

Lesson 6: Kindness

The fifth fruit of the Spirit is *kindness*. Kindness is not just about treating people right; it is also about focusing on the needs of others and treating others with respect from a grateful heart. Kindness is not just something we do—it is a lifestyle.

Here again, God taught us that we did not know as much as we thought we did. We did not realize that there was a deeper meaning to the type of kindness that Jesus asks of us. You may have thought the same as us: that being kind was smiling at someone, saying hello, holding open a door, or being polite. And it is good to do those things. But the word that the Greeks used for kindness (*chrēstotēs*) took kindness a lot further. The definition of this word is as follows: "moral goodness, integrity, kindness" (Thayer and Smith, 1999). This is a kindness that we do not just engage in from time to time. We like how Pastor Stephen Witmer described it. "It's a supernaturally generous orientation of our hearts toward other people, even when they don't deserve it and don't love us in return" (Witmer, 2016).

Let us start by discussing the greatest kindness ever shown. When Jesus died on the cross, He demonstrated extreme kindness for us. We don't often associate His sacrifice with kindness, but it truly is the ultimate act of kindness. Doing something sacrificial for the sake of others without expecting to be repaid is the exact definition of what Jesus did for us on the cross.

Authentic kindness can only come from the Holy Spirit. As we've mentioned, abiding with God orients our hearts with His heart. When we abide in Him on a regular basis, His kindness will flow through us and we have a different relationship with others as a result. We will find ourselves showing kindness to others whether they deserve it or not. "Whoever pursues righteousness and love finds life, prosperity, and honor" (Proverbs 21:21).

Kindness also has another purpose other than just reflecting God's character. Genuine kindness will lead others to repentance. In Romans 2, Paul is talking about how people have no excuse to judge others because we all have the same sins. He is saying that to judge someone else (instead of showing kindness) we are ultimately judging ourselves because we are all sinners. He asks a rhetorical question in verse 3: "So when you, a mere human being, pass judgment on them and yet do the same things, do you think you will escape God's judgment?" Bottom line: We are all God's children and, rather than passing judgment, we should go out of our way to express authentic kindness to everyone, because that's what God does.

Paul continues to ask in verse 4, "Or do you show contempt for the riches of His kindness, forbearance, and patience, not realizing that God's kindness is intended to lead you to repentance?" God's kindness is having Jesus die on the cross for us so that we can be reconciled to Him and live with Him for eternity. When we represent authentic kindness without judgment toward others, there is a chance that we can help lead them to repentance or that a seed will be planted that will ultimately lead them to Christ.

Once again, we are unable to show this sort of kindness toward others on our own. Our human nature is not bent toward being genuinely kind regardless of the cost to ourselves. It is only by abiding in Christ that we are able to allow His Spirit to flow through us, showing God's kindness to others.

Look deep inside your heart and ask yourself this question: Are you more focused on seeking to serve others in genuine kindness or are you content with showing politeness and "surface" kindness?

_____

_____

_____

_____

What would it look like if you were to show genuine kindness to someone you don't feel deserves it? Make a concerted effort to ask God for His help in showing His kindness.

_____

_____

_____

_____

Lesson 7: Goodness

We throw the word *good* around frequently. We say "I'm good" when asked how we are doing. We associate anything positive with being good. *Goodness* is often described as the act of being good or nice. While that is true, it is only part of the story. Like the other fruit we have studied thus far, goodness goes much deeper. It is not so much of an action as much as it is an attitude that spurs us to action. Goodness is a characteristic of God. The Bible states very clearly that

God is good. "You are good, and what you do is good; teach me your decrees" (Psalm 119:68)

Also, like the other fruits we have studied, we are unable to produce the type of goodness God asks of us on our own power. The only way we can display God's goodness is to abide in Him and allow the Holy Spirit to manifest a disposition of goodness in our character. Oh, y'all, we have been hit by that train again! We have been convicted by the Holy Spirit with every stroke of the keyboard and every added page! We did not have any idea of the depth of the type of goodness being described in the Bible.

When we share in the character of God and show goodness, we are inspired to do the right thing even when it is difficult. We want to do the right and good thing, even if the crowd is doing something different. That isn't always easy to do! (Can we get an AMEN?) When we consider what God did for us, as the ultimate demonstration of goodness, just so we could be saved, we realize how difficult it was for Him! But He did it anyway. He sent His only son to be beaten, nailed to a cross, and to ultimately die so He could overcome sin and we can be reconciled to Him. That is the supreme example of showing genuine goodness. So we ask You to teach us Your goodness, God!

There are many examples of goodness in the Bible. We are sure that many of you have heard the story of the Good Samaritan in Luke 10:30–35. We tend to gloss over this story and think that it's nice that the Samaritan helped the man, but let's dive a bit deeper.

Here is the story: A Jewish man was going to Jericho and was attacked, beaten, and stripped by robbers on his way. The robbers left him naked and wounded on the side of the road to die. A priest and a Levite both passed by the man on the other side of the road doing nothing to help him. A Samaritan (who was hated by the Jews because of his nationality) stopped to help this man. He treated his wounds and placed the beaten man on his donkey. He took him to an inn and stayed with him overnight. In the morning, he instructed the innkeeper to take care of the injured man and gave the innkeeper two days' wages for his trouble. He also promised to return to reimburse the innkeeper for any more expenses he may incur.

Let us first look at the priest and the Levite who ignored the injured man. They "obviously" had something important to do. Perhaps they were running late to work. Maybe the wife had dinner on the stove. Or they needed to get to their child's school event. There could have been urgent and valid excuses for them to keep going. Of course, it is possible that they were just being selfish and did not want to help.

We must admit that we too have done the same at some point in our lives. We have chosen to not do the right and good thing when something was happening, or we saw something that we did not want to get involved in. It could have been something small, like not opening the door for someone whose hands were full. Or, it could have been a bigger event, like noticing that someone needed help and instead we turned away. We all (including the priest and the Levite) have missed opportunities to do the good and right thing, despite it being hard. This is what God wants us to notice about ourselves.

What opportunities to do the good and right thing have you missed? (Be honest.)

_____

_____

_____

_____

Now that we have talked about the wrong thing to do, let us get to the good news. The Samaritan was facing many obstacles in his choice to help. The Samaritan knew that the injured man would not like him simply because he was a Samaritan. But he did NOT let that stop him from doing good. He had genuine goodness in his heart. The

Bible says "And when he saw him, he took pity on him" (Luke 10:33). Other versions say that he had compassion for him.

The Samaritan could see that this man was in terrible shape and was barely clinging to life. He could have thought he was beyond help, but he stopped to tend to the man's wounds anyway. He poured oil and wine on them and then bandaged them. Oil and wine were not cheap commodities, and this Samaritan probably did not have a cellar full. He did not let that stop him from choosing to do good.

He took the man to an inn and gave instructions to the innkeeper to watch after him. That cost money. He gave the innkeeper two days' wages and promised to pay back any other expenses. It is more than likely that this man was not rich. It is more than likely that he did not have a lot of extra money to put toward caring for this man. This was turning out to be a very expensive endeavor! Once again, he didn't let that stop him.

Unfortunately, this is where the story ends. We do not know if that man who was beaten and robbed ended up living or dying. We do not know if the Samaritan was thanked for all of his kindnesses. We do not know how much the Samaritan ended up spending in all. We do not know if the wounded man was permanently scarred or healed completely. We do not know if they became lifetime friends or never spoke again. All we know is that this Samaritan chose to do the good and right thing no matter what obstacles he faced.

Imagine if someone who has been unkind or unfair to you in the past needed serious help and God gave you the opportunity to care for them. Could you say that you would be able to step up and do the good and right thing? This very question has caused us to take a pause and check our hearts.

Our challenge to you is to pray for those opportunities to show goodness to others. No matter how big or how small, genuine goodness will always be the right thing to do. And we cannot do it without God's help.

As Christians, we all do "good" things. What is the motive behind your actions? Have you allowed the goodness of the Holy Spirit to spur you to action? Do you do good things because it is expected of you, or it looks good to others? Or, do you do good things because you know it is the right thing to do, no matter how difficult? Take time to really think and reflect. Can you do better? We know we can, and we will.

_____

_____

_____

_____

Lesson 8: Faithfulness

Faithful can be defined as "full of faith." In chapter 1, we discussed faith as being an action step to abiding, placing our faith in God alone. The closer we get to God, the stronger our faith becomes. Not surprisingly, faith is also a fruit of the Spirit. Most modern translations use the word *faithfulness* but in the King James Version, it is simply listed as *faith*. There is another way to view faithfulness, which is what we will address in this section. Throughout this guide, we have talked about the fruit of the Spirit as God's character traits. Our God is certainly faithful!

Of course, when we seek to be faithful, we look to the perfecter of faithfulness, God Himself. Numerous times in the Bible we read about God's faithfulness and many verses assure us of God's faithfulness to us.

1. **2 Thessalonians 3:3**—"But the Lord is faithful, and He will strengthen you and protect you from the evil one."
2. **1 John 1:9**— "If we confess our sins, He is faithful and just and will forgive us our sins and purify us from all unrighteousness."
3. **Deuteronomy 7:9**—"Know therefore that the Lord your God is God; He is the faithful God, keeping His covenant of love to a thousand generations of those who love Him and keep His commandments."

Those are just a few of the many verses that speak of the faithfulness of God. God will never leave us or forsake us. He will always "have our backs" and be there for us. Even when we may not see Him, He is near. If you haven't been spending a lot of time with Him, it might be hard to see His hand on your life. Abiding brings it all into focus. The more we abide, the more we can clearly see His involvement with us.

We challenge you to look back and write down a time where you can clearly see God's faithfulness in your life.

_____

_____

_____

_____

Just as with the other fruits of the Spirit, we must abide so that God can grow and deepen our faithfulness.

Consider for a moment the meaning of Matthew 25:21. "His master replied, 'Well done, good and faithful servant! You have been faithful with a few things; I will put you in charge of many things. Come and share your master's happiness!'" Part of that verse states,

"Well done, good and faithful servant!" The parable surrounding that verse talks about a man who was going on a trip, and he entrusted his money to his three servants while he was gone. The man seems to be mean and dishonest, but the Bible compares this man's servants to us (God's servants).

We find the story starting in Matthew 25:14. The master who leaves gives one servant five bags of gold, two bags to another servant, and one bag to the third servant. While he was gone, the first servant used his gifts and doubled the master's money, ending up with ten bags total. The second servant did the same, ending up with four bags total. However, the third servant who was afraid of his master hid the money in the ground and did not increase the amount.

The master returned from his trip and the first two servants presented him with the original amount of money along with the money gained during his departure. The third servant fearfully presented his master with the original bag of money. "Then the man who had received one bag of gold came. 'Master,' he said, 'I knew that you are a hard man, harvesting where you have not sown and gathering where you have not scattered seed. So I was afraid and went out and hid your gold in the ground. See, here is what belongs to you'" (Matthew 25:24–25).

After the first two servants had shown their master what they had been able to do with the money, he praised them both greatly. However, he had an unpleasantly harsh response for the third servant.

> "His master replied, 'You wicked, lazy servant! So you knew that I harvest where I have not sown and gather where I have not scattered seed? Well then, you should have put my money on deposit with the bankers, so that when I returned I would have received it back with interest. So take the bag of gold from him and give it to the one who has ten bags. For

whoever has will be given more, and they will have an abundance. Whoever does not have, even what they have will be taken from them. And throw that worthless servant outside, into the darkness, where there will be weeping and gnashing of teeth'" (Matthew 25:26–30).

WOW! While we know that our God is loving and caring, we also need to know that our God is Truth. And that truth will sometimes be harsh. He will be honest about what we have done and whether it pleases Him or not. Like the master in the parable, God expects us to take the gifts we are given and use them to multiply His Kingdom. These gifts are not strictly limited to our finances. While utilizing our money to spread His Word is important, we also have other gifts we can put to work for God. We all have time, talents, strengths, and spiritual gifts that we are given to help share His Word and love. When we do this, we will hear what the first two servants were able to hear. "You have been faithful with a few things; I will put you in charge of many things. Come and share your master's happiness!" Isn't that what we all want to hear at the end of our journey? *Well done my good and faithful servant!*

From the time that I (Stephanie) heard that verse, it has become a goal and a dream to hear God whisper those words to me. I live for the day when He tells me that I've done a good job for Him and that He is pleased with me. I can't imagine a bigger or better compliment than the Creator of everything telling little me that I've done well. The closer I've become to Him, the more I want to please Him. However, I cannot please Him unless I commit to being faithful. And the only way He can cultivate that fruit in me is when I abide in Him.

When we show God that we can be good stewards and utilize the resources and talents He bestows upon us, He is then able to entrust us with even more. He is pleased with our return on His investment.

In what ways are you applying the resources, gifts, and talents that God has given you to expand His Kingdom?

_____

_____

_____

_____

Are there any resources, gifts, or talents that you are not currently using for the glory of God? If so, how can you put those into practice?

_____

_____

_____

_____

Lesson 9: Gentleness

What would you think if we told you that *gentleness* can be described as "strength under control" (Morris, 2019)? That isn't typically a phrase that comes to mind when we envision gentleness, is it? Go ahead, give it a try. Think of someone in your life who you would consider embodying gentleness. What traits do you see?

If your image was anything like ours tends to be, it was a picture of soft-spoken people who are sweet and kind and get walked all over by others. You might think of gentleness as weakness. You might think that a gentle person is powerless and not strong enough to stand up against strife. Even the dictionary says that the word *gentle* means "kindly; amiable; not severe, rough, or violent; mild; moderate; gradual" (Dictionary.com, 2021).

Whereas that could be true for someone who is not abiding in Christ, *gentleness* means something entirely different for those who trust in God. True gentleness can be described in one word . . . *Jesus*.

When we read about how Jesus conducted Himself in the Bible, He was the epitome of gentleness. And we know with 100% certainty that He was not weak! There are numerous stories in the Bible about how He responded to people with gentleness. One such story talks about Jesus at the last Passover meal with His disciples. In John 13:5–38, we read about Jesus turning the tables and washing the disciples' feet. He already knew that He was about to be betrayed by Judas and denied three times by Peter and yet He performed a duty for His disciples that was typically reserved for servants.

In John 8, we read about a woman who was caught in adultery and who was going to be stoned by the Pharisees. Jesus' response to the Pharisees was gentle, yet convincing. "When they kept on questioning Him, He straightened up and said to them, 'Let any one of you who is without sin be the first to throw a stone at her'" (verse 7). Likewise, His response to the woman was equally gentle. He said (verse 11), "Then neither do I condemn you . . . Go now and leave your life of sin." He did not ignore the fact that sin was present in her life, but He did not chastise her.

The fourth chapter of John, verses 1–42, tell us another story about Jesus' gentleness. Jesus and His disciples traveled through Samaria and stopped by a well for a drink because they were tired. There was a woman there gathering water. The Jews were not supposed to interact with Samaritans at all, and yet Jesus asked this woman for a drink. After she expressed her shock that He was even speaking to her, He began to talk with her about the Living Water. He tells her to go get her husband and she admits that she is not married. Jesus calmly confirms that He already knew about her situation and past husbands. The woman believed that He was the Messiah and ended up telling many about Him, thereby causing more to believe in Jesus. Jesus did not gloss over the truth of her situation. While He acknowledged her sin, He was still gentle and loving.

Jesus never backed down from His Truth in any situation. In the Bible, He spoke God's Word with honesty and confidence and never wavered. The amazing thing is that He did this without being aggressive.

What if Jesus had judged the woman at the well? What if He had put her down, ridiculed her, and called her names? What if He had harshly criticized her actions? How do you think the woman would have responded if He had? Do you think that many people would have ended up placing their trust in Him? Do you think that the Truth of the Gospel would have been spread and shared that day?

Let's circle back to the story in John 8 about the adulteress. The Pharisees wanted to stone her because of her sin. When they asked Jesus what to do, He could have said, "Go ahead!" He could have condemned her and sealed her fate as well. What kind of example would have been set that day if He had responded like this? Would the true nature of God's love have been revealed?

Think about how we respond to others. Has being rude and judgmental ever helped a conversation to go well? Jesus knew this. He knew that people do not respond well to harsh and hurtful attitudes. Jesus' gentle responses in all these stories not only helped to save the lives of a lot of people but set the example for us to follow.

Jesus is described as "the gentle Shepherd." Isaiah 40:11 says, "He tends His flock like a shepherd: He gathers the lambs in His arms and carries them close to His heart; He **gently** leads those that have young" (emphasis added). Jesus Himself even tells us that He is gentle! In Matthew 11:28–30, He says, "Come to Me, all you who are weary and burdened, and I will give you rest. Take My yoke upon you and learn from Me, for I am **gentle** and humble in heart, and you will find rest for your souls. For My yoke is easy and My burden is light" (emphasis added).

Christianity gets a bad rap because many Christians tend to be judgmental and ugly toward others. Even if they are not being directly hateful to someone, the things that are posted on social media can still sting the person who is reading. It is no surprise that people are watching Christians to see how they will respond to others or to a situation. Colossians 4:5–6 states, "Be wise in the way you act toward outsiders; make the most of every opportunity. Let your conversation be always full of grace, seasoned with salt, so that you may know how to answer everyone."

We are to stand up for and defend God's Truth, but we are to do it with kind, loving words and attitudes, speaking the Truth with love. We are not to pacify others by saying what they want to hear to make them feel better. We are called to share the Gospel the way it is presented in the Bible, not altering God's Word.

But we cannot do this when we are criticizing others' choices or belittling them for their opinions. If you have ever had someone make fun of you or judge you for your values, then you know that it does not exactly make you want to see things from their point of view. "A gentle answer turns away wrath, but a harsh word stirs up anger" (Proverbs 15:1).

When we encounter someone who doesn't know Christ or has opposing opinions, we are to respond with understanding and grace. "Gracious words are a honeycomb, sweet to the soul and healing to the bones" (Proverbs 16:24). We are to tell them the Truth gently and lovingly. They might not agree with us. They might laugh at our beliefs. They could turn and walk away. But, when we are respectfully sharing the Gospel, seeds are being planted. Others will recall when we shared our beliefs in a way that didn't mock or insult them. Philippians 4:5 instructs us to "let your gentleness be evident to all. The Lord is near." "Therefore, as God's chosen people, holy and dearly loved, clothe yourselves with compassion, kindness, humility, **gentleness,** and patience" (Colossians 3:12 emphasis added). In Ephesians 4:2, "Be completely humble and **gentle**; be patient, bearing with one another in love" (emphasis added).

Basically, God calls for us to be bold and gentle at the same time. He wants us to follow His example. In 1 Peter 3:15, we read, "But in your hearts revere Christ as Lord. Always be prepared to give an answer to everyone who asks you to give the reason for the hope that you have. **But do this with gentleness and respect**" (emphasis added).

Take some time to write what you would say in response to anyone who asks you the reason for your hope in Christ. What would you say while being gentle and bold at the same time?

_____

_____

_____

_____

Sometimes we disagree with people in positions of power, such as political leaders, church leaders, or work bosses. Sometimes we also disagree with imposed rules or laws. We can easily get angry if we feel that others are trying to threaten our freedoms or take away our rights. This is a sensitive topic because often we believe we are justified in our harsh responses to these situations. But read Titus 3:1–2, "Remind the people to be subject to rulers and authorities, to be obedient, to be ready to do whatever is good, to slander no one, to be peaceable and considerate, and always to be gentle toward everyone." We are not being asked to back down from our beliefs, but to be gentle no matter the circumstance.

If you find yourself in a situation where you disagree with leadership or laws or rules, how can you display a gentle response using controlled strength?

_____

_____

_____

_____

Lesson 10: Self-Control

According to a weekly devotional from Grand Canyon University, *self-control* is the ability "to resist temptation and avoid conforming to the things of this world" (Abraham, 2016). Dictionary.com defines *self-control* as "control or restraint of oneself or one's actions, feelings, etc." (2021).

Having read these definitions, it almost seems as if God is not involved in this fruit of the Spirit but that could not be more wrong. Typically, self-control is looked at as something that we are expected to have innately. We have the ability to control our choices and our lives, right? Instead, self-control is very hard to possess without Jesus' help! Trying to resist temptation or restrain your emotions is a massive struggle without the aid of the Holy Spirit. We believe this is why Jesus lists it with the other fruits. As a matter of fact, self-control, or the lack thereof, shows up in every other fruit.

Self-control is like the bow on the fruit basket. It ties it all together in a pretty little package. Without self-control, it is extremely difficult to demonstrate the other fruits. Think of it this way: We can **react** to situations by allowing our earthly emotions to dictate what we say or do; or, we can carefully **respond** by choosing our words and actions according to the expectations of Jesus. We cannot choose to show love to someone who has offended us without self-control. We cannot choose to show patience with someone who is testing us without self-control. Get the idea?

Listen to what Paul says in Romans 7:18. "For I know that good itself does not dwell in me, that is, in my sinful nature. For I have the desire to do what is good, but I cannot carry it out." We encourage you to read the entire passage, Romans 7:7–25. Paul describes a struggle that we all have. In our own power, we have a hard time choosing to do the right thing. This is why we need the Holy Spirit to guide us and help us in exhibiting self-control.

We all make or have made poor choices out of a lack of self-control in response to someone or something. We know we have! We have all said the wrong thing or acted in a way that was inappropriate. When this happens, we have several choices. We either take responsibility for our actions, pretend it didn't happen, justify what we've done, or pass the blame for why we did it. This last option seems to be the most popular. We have blamed it on our circumstances, tying it to how stressed we were. We have blamed it on someone else, claiming that they were pushing all our buttons. We have blamed our childhood for creating these unhealthy behaviors in us. The list could go on and on.

It is all too easy to blame someone or something else when we act in a manner unbecoming. As a matter of fact, that is one of the first things we read about in the Bible. *Blame for a misdeed.* We have all read the story in Genesis about Adam and Eve and the directive from God to not eat of the tree of the knowledge of good and evil. We all remember how Eve was tricked by the serpent to go ahead and take a bite Then, of course, she convinces Adam to eat the fruit as well. When asked why they ate from the tree, Adam blames God and Eve and then Eve blames the serpent. In Genesis 3:12–13, "The man said, 'The woman You put here with me—she gave me some fruit from the tree, and I ate it.' Then the Lord God said to the woman, 'What is this you have done?' The woman said, 'The serpent deceived me, and I ate.'"

What have been some of your excuses for your actions? Be honest!

_____

_____

_____

_____

In addition, self-control is not about us controlling our own lives, contrary to popular belief. We are to submit to God's control and guidance. While He gives us free will and we have the option to "take the wheel," our own paths will lead us to destruction.

We live in a world that emphasizes SELF. Everywhere we look, we see strategies for self-care, books and articles on self-help and self-improvement, tendencies toward self-reliance, and encouragement to achieve self-fulfillment. The one thing that all of these have in common is the focus on SELF. We need to be careful about the type of "self" stuff we allow to enter our lives.

In a slideshow from Ameerah Lewis on the website Slideshare .net, we read how this focus on self is a tactic straight from the devil (Lewis, 2013). He knows how impactful we are when we rely on God and His power. The devil wants us to become less reliant on God so that he can take us down with him and so that we won't bring others to Christ. Her graphic shows a good representation of how we can get stuck in a cycle of putting trust in ourselves and not trusting God. She shares that if the devil can keep us controlling our own lives, without God's help, he can keep us failing. If we continue to fail, we will continue to feel guilt and shame. If he can keep us feeling guilty and shameful, he can keep us from asking God for help. If he can keep us from asking God for help, he can keep us controlling our own lives. Thus, the cycle repeats.

We think the cycle that Lewis presents describes precisely how the devil tries to keep us focused on ourselves. And in today's society, how easy it is to fall into this trap!

While we have our own choices in life, our spiritual self-control should guide the decisions that we make. There is a point to be made here. While giving God control is paramount, we also need to take time to take care of ourselves. This is different from the type of "self-care" the world promotes. In this type of self-care, we turn to God for help in caring for our bodies and souls. We need adequate rest and nutrition. We need relationships with others and the community. We need to take time to abide in Jesus and refill our spiritual cups. God created us to need all those things and there is nothing wrong with seeking Him to help us with fulfilling those needs.

Above all else, it is imperative to make sure that we are surrendering to God for control. We look to Him for guidance in decisions (both big and small) and ask Him to help us maintain self-control in all aspects of our life.

Let us examine Romans 12:1–2. "Therefore, I urge you, brothers and sisters, in view of God's mercy, to offer your bodies as a living sacrifice, holy and pleasing to God—this is your true and proper worship. Do not conform to the pattern of this world, but be transformed by the renewing of your mind. Then you will be able to test and approve what God's will is—his good, pleasing and perfect will." This passage is reminding us how we are to allow God, not the world, to transform our minds. We are to conform to God's will.

Ephesians 4:22–24 reiterates that passage in Romans. "You were taught, with regard to your former way of life, to put off your old self, which is being corrupted by its deceitful desires; to be made new in the attitude of your minds; and to put on the new self, created to be like God in true righteousness and holiness." This passage reminds us that our *old self*, the self we had before we surrendered to Christ, is easily corrupted and that we need to allow God to recreate us.

Take a moment to consider the connection of self-control to the other fruits. How can you purposefully seek God's aid in bolstering your self-control in showing love? In spreading and having joy? In maintaining peace? In demonstrating patience? In sharing kindness? In depicting goodness? In displaying faithfulness? In achieving gentleness?

_____

_____

_____

_____

What reminders do you need to place in your life to ensure that you are turning to Him so that you can live out all of the fruits of the Spirit?

_____

_____

_____

_____

CHAPTER 3

WAITING

Sometimes *abiding* means waiting. On the surface, waiting doesn't seem like it has much to do with abiding. After all, we want to go and do things for the Lord. We want to be used by Him. We want our faith to accomplish something. We want to fill dry bones with life!

Let us say that these are not bad desires to have! We desire those things ourselves. And while it is healthy to want the Lord to use us to further His kingdom, we must look at those moments in our lives when God tells us to wait.

In the books of Exodus and Numbers, we read the story of Moses leading his people out of Egypt. Most of us are familiar with this story: Moses demanding the freedom of the Israelites and the Pharaoh letting them go after hundreds of years of captivity. Moses led the people into the desert, and they were guided by God who appeared as a pillar of cloud by day and a pillar of fire by night.

Something that we never knew about this story was that God had the Israelites wait on multiple occasions. In Exodus 40:34, we are told that God descended upon the tabernacle in the form of a cloud. "Then the cloud covered the tent of meeting, and the glory of the Lord filled the tabernacle." As we read further in Exodus, chapter 40, we see that when that cloud was hovering over the tabernacle, the Israelites were not to travel. Verses 36–37 say, "In all the travels of the Israelites, whenever the cloud lifted from above the tabernacle, they would set out; but if the cloud did not lift, they did not set out—until the day it lifted." It is spoken about again in Numbers 9:16–17. Those Scriptures tell us: "That is how it continued to be; the cloud covered it, and at night it looked like fire. Whenever the cloud lifted from above the tent, the Israelites set out; wherever the cloud settled, the Israelites encamped."

We are never told the reason God had them wait to travel, but we can surmise that He wanted them to remain focused on Him.

The word *wait* when it is referring to waiting on the Lord, is the Hebrew word *qavah*. *Qavah* means (1) "to bind together" (perhaps by twisting strands as in making a rope), (2) "look patiently," (3) "tarry or wait," and (4) "hope, expect, look eagerly" (Keathley, 2004). *Waiting* can also mean being silent.

There are two different versions of waiting. There is passive waiting and active waiting. *Passive waiting* is when we sit back, kick our feet up, and wait for something to happen. In passive waiting, we are tempted to rush ahead with our own desires instead of waiting for God's answer. *Active waiting* is when we actively seek God through prayer and reading the Word of God. When we actively wait, we abide in Christ and remain close enough to hear His call.

Lesson 1: Reasons for Waiting

Section 1: Resting

In chapter 1, we shared some of the definitions of the word *abide*. Other definitions of the word *abide* are "to wait; to pause; to delay" and "to wait for; to be prepared for; to await; to watch for" (Webster-dictionary.net). When we apply these definitions to our walk with Christ, we can clearly see that there will be moments of resting and waiting.

Let us explore one of the ways waiting might look while we are abiding. Think about an athlete who pushes their body to, and often past, its limits. A runner or a swimmer in a race, a football player during a game, or a weightlifter in a competition, to name a few. In order to utilize their bodies at maximum capacity, they must rest before and after events. They must get adequate sleep to replenish their strength so that their muscles can perform at their peak. If an athlete were to perform in event after event with no rest, their body would exhaust all of its energy and shut down. Muscles need time to prepare, and muscles need time to recover and repair. The same can be said for our spiritual muscles.

Take a quick look at your cell phone, laptop, or another electronic device. When it runs out of battery power, what do you do? You plug it in to recharge the battery. Once the battery dies, that device becomes useless. The same can be said for us and our relationship with God. If we do not take time to slow down, quiet ourselves, and wait on Him, we miss the opportunity to get recharged and renewed. Our batteries run out and we become susceptible to the devil's schemes. Without rest, we are not able to gain the strength to do the work of the Lord.

If we are out doing and going for God on a consistent basis and not slowing down to wait and replenish, our energy will be depleted. We will not be effective in completing God's work. We are not saying that acting in the name of the Lord is a bad thing, but it is important to listen for God's will in our actions. And we need to remember that God has also called us to wait on and rest in Him.

"But those who wait on the LORD Shall renew their strength; they shall mount up with wings like eagles, they shall run and not be weary, they shall walk and not faint" (Isaiah 40:31; KJV).

Many of us are familiar with this passage. Chris Tomlin has written a song about it ("Everlasting God"). We return to this passage when we are weary and need to remind ourselves of God's strength. However, we often overlook the part where it talks about those who **WAIT** on the Lord receiving His strength. Yes, God gives us strength.

But think about how much strength we could have when we sit still, wait, and allow God to fill our souls.

Waiting and being still is not easy, we know. It is hard to be quiet with the Lord and try to shut out the things around us. It is hard to hush the screams of the world and tune into the whisper of Jesus. But it is essential for us to do this because this is when our spirit and energy will be restored by Him. We can pray and ask Him to speak clearly through the clutter of our thoughts so that we will know it is Him. We do not always need to be asking for things or doing all of the talking during our prayer time. It is okay to sit in silence, with openness to God's voice, and allow Him to speak to you.

Have you ever taken time to just sit still and wait on God? If yes, describe how your strength may have been renewed during that time. If not, what do you think might happen if you took some time to just be still?

_____

_____

_____

_____

Section 2: Expecting Answers

Another form of waiting might look like waiting on God to answer our prayers. We have been told that God always answers our prayers. And He does! The Bible tells us in Mark 11:24, "Therefore I tell you, whatever you ask for in prayer, believe that you have received it, and it will be yours." Of course, at times, God will answer *yes* or *no* immediately, but that is not the only way He answers us. There is something we refer to as "unanswered prayers" that are not really unanswered prayers. Sometimes God's answer is WAIT. That answer is the hardest of the three to accept. We live in a world of instant gratification and waiting is not our specialty. We want God to act right now. However, God has His own timing, and we know that His timing is perfect. We might be praying for something that He does, in fact, have in store for us, but not for several months or years down the road. In those cases, His answer is *to wait*. He might tell us *to wait* when we are seeking guidance for a decision or direction. He might tell us *to wait* when we are desiring to obtain something in our lives.

For example, a young couple might want to buy a house shortly after they are married. But God knows that, in a year, the husband will be getting a significant raise at work and, until then, they cannot comfortably afford a house payment. While they are out searching for a house, they might run into roadblock after roadblock because God is saying WAIT.

Another example is a young lady who is praying for God to send her the husband He intends for her. She might be praying that her current boyfriend will propose so they can start their lives together. However, God may have another man whom He intends for her to marry and is telling her to WAIT.

We both have experienced this in our own lives when it pertained to our careers. We both prayed and prayed for the just-right teaching job. We both had numerous interviews. And we both were facing rejection after rejection. What we know now (but did not know then) is that God had our careers planned out and He was telling both of us to WAIT.

Consider for a moment that your wait might be due to a spiritual battle within the unseen realm. In the Bible, we are told about Daniel and how he prayed and fasted for 21 days to receive an answer from the Lord (Daniel 10:2–3). Later in the chapter, his answer arrives but there is a shocking message with it. Verses 12–14 of chapter 10 tell us how the angel sent to answer his prayer was dispatched right away. God immediately heard his first prayer. Then, the angel was delayed by a messenger of darkness for 21 days. The angel was finally able to get to Daniel after another angel, Michael, helped him get past the dark forces. Daniel did not give up! He continued to pray during those 21 days. God hears our prayers immediately, even if the answer takes longer than we expect.

When we think that we know more than God, we are headed for trouble. We are not saying that any of us actually think that we know more than God, but when we rush ahead without listening to the voice of the Lord, our actions are saying that we can plan our lives better than He can. We cannot. Too many times we have made decisions based on our own understanding and desires. Proverbs 3:5–6 reminds us: "Trust in the Lord with all your heart and lean not on your own understanding; in all your ways submit to Him, and He will make your paths straight."

We need to rely on the prompting and voice of the Holy Spirit to guide us. So, what if we hear nothing from God? What if He seems silent? Sometimes, what we do not hear is Him telling us to wait.

Think back on your life's journey so far. Have there been moments where God seemed silent, absent, or simply not moving? Describe one of those moments here.

_____

_____

_____

_____

As you reflect on that moment of your life, was it possibly instead a time of God telling you to wait?

"'For I know the plans I have for you,' declares the Lord, 'plans to prosper you and not to harm you, plans to give you hope and a future. Then you will call on Me and come and pray to Me, and I will listen to you. You will seek Me and find Me when you seek Me with all your heart'" (Jeremiah 29:11–13).

Section 3: Changes

Many times, our waiting is actually God making changes within us. God has wonderful blessings in store for us but before He can hand them over, we need to let go of what is unhealthy for us or allow for some changes within us. If our hands are full of the things we think we need, we cannot grasp the much better things God has waiting for us. If we think that we are not in need of improvement, then we cannot allow God to transform us into the person He intends us to be.

In his blog for *FaithGateway*, Pete Wilson states, "Spiritual transformation doesn't take place when we get what we want. It takes place while we're waiting. It is forged in us while we're waiting, hoping, and trusting, even though we have yet to receive what we long for. Spiritual transformation happens in the waiting room" (Wilson, 2015).

How many times have we clung to the things that we think are keeping us afloat, when in actuality, they are weights causing us to sink? God is our life preserver, and He is waiting for us to let go of those weights. Yes, we said that He is waiting for us to let go. He waits on us, too. What He wants to place in our hands will pull us out of the choppy waters and place us on solid ground, if only we will let go.

Isaiah 43:18–19 tells us, "Forget the former things; do not dwell on the past. See, I am doing a new thing! Now it springs up; do you not perceive it? I am making a way in the wilderness and streams in the wasteland."

God also uses waiting time to heal our wounds and strengthen our souls. We are flawed, bruised, and battered. We have allowed ourselves, at one time or another, to believe the lies of the devil. Sometimes, we need healing before we are ready for the gifts God wants to bestow upon us. If we cannot see through the lies and fear, then we cannot receive the blessings God has waiting for us.

We might need some time of restoration and growth so that we can truly appreciate God's blessing. We have found that in the writing of this study, we have become much more open to what God wants to do in our lives because of what we have learned. Perhaps someone needs time to heal from a broken relationship before they can pour themselves into another one, even if it is the relationship God has waiting for them. Possibly, someone needs to learn some life lessons before they are able to impart on the career God wishes them to have. We often pray for God to remove us from a bad situation. It could be that God needs someone to walk through a tough experience so that they can later minister to others. Perhaps we need to adopt an attitude of humility and let go of our selfish, self-centered selves before we can be a servant in God's kingdom. These are all times of waiting.

Think of a time when God made you wait on something so that He could heal you or prepare you for something better. How did you respond to that wait time?

_____

_____

_____

_____

Looking back on that moment now, were you able to heal or let go of what was weighing you down? What blessing did you receive from God in its place?

_____

_____

_____

_____

Lesson 2: What We Gain from Waiting

Waiting on God can be difficult and frustrating. We want what we want when we want it. It is important to remember that God's timing is perfect and that He is working while we wait. Even if we cannot see or feel Him, He continues to work on our behalf. We gain so many things when we take time to wait upon God!

1. **Rest**—We spoke about resting as being a reason that God has us wait, but rest is also something we gain when we wait. So often we look at waiting as a luxury we do not have time for. But resting rejuvenates our mind, body, and spirit. Once we give it to God, we can rest in the fact that He is in control and will take care of us.

2. **Patience**—Oh, how we struggle with being patient! We are so used to getting almost everything instantly that patience has practically become obsolete. Think about how you feel if a web page takes longer than 10 seconds to load. Been there? We have! We tap our feet and whisper, "Come on, come on." But patience is a gift that we can receive when we slow down and WAIT. God grants us the ability to put on the brakes and appreciate what He has done. "Be patient, then, brothers and sisters, until the Lord's

coming. See how the farmer waits for the land to yield its valuable crop, patiently waiting for the autumn and spring rains. You too, be patient and stand firm, because the Lord's coming is near" (James 5:7–8).

3. **Humility**—Waiting on God allows us to see Him as He truly is: majestic and full of glory. When we humble ourselves and let God take control, we are able to see ourselves from the correct perspective. We can take time to marvel at how all-encompassing He is and bask in His love for us. We serve a mighty, mighty God! Humility allows us to wait for God's best. We are tempted to take matters into our own hands, running ahead of what God has planned for us. However, when we do that, we miss out. We miss out on the humility that comes with trusting His perspective instead of our limited viewpoint.

4. **Exposure of Our Motives**—This might not seem like a blessing of waiting at first; but, in reality, having the truth about our motives revealed allows us to set our own agendas aside and submit to the will of God. We should always ask for God's will to be done in every situation, without asking for what WE think should be done. We learn how to desire Him, instead of just a quick resolution to our problems.

5. **Trust and Faith**—Waiting for God to move requires an exorbitant amount of trust and faith. We must believe that God will do what He says He will do. While we wait, we should wait expectantly in faith. God will answer! And you never know, perhaps God is waiting for you to WAIT. "The Lord is good to those whose hope is in Him, to the one who seeks Him; it is good to wait quietly for the salvation of the Lord" (Lamentations 3:25–26).

6. **Blessings**—God loves to shower us with gifts and blessings. He loves to give good things to His children. When we wait upon Him, He has the opportunity to bestow those gifts upon us because we are able to give Him the glory. If He is telling us to wait, it might be because He has something bigger and better in store

for us. "Blessed is the one who perseveres under trial because, having stood the test, that person will receive the crown of life that the Lord has promised to those who love Him" (James 1:12).

7. **Protection**—When we wait on God, He then protects us from the consequences, and possible danger, of our impulsive choices. We are able to listen to that small whisper of the Holy Spirit and He is able to guide us and leads us into decisions that honor Him. "We wait in hope for the Lord; He is our help and our shield" (Psalm 33:20).

8. **Wisdom**—If we spend our waiting time abiding, studying His Word, and praying, we will gain His wisdom and His clarity. It is a guarantee. You cannot spend time with God and not come out wiser. "If any of you lacks wisdom, you should ask God, who gives generously to all without finding fault, and it will be given to you" (James 1:5).

While this list is not all-inclusive, it gives you a good idea of the amazing gifts that we receive when we wait upon the Lord. Can you see how waiting on Him is so much better than rushing ahead and making hasty decisions? We know how hard it is to wait. It is human nature to give up during the waiting. We can easily start to feel that God has forsaken us or left us hanging. We question God's love and sometimes His existence. The good news is that you are not alone while you wait! God will be with you, strengthening you, and rewarding your persistence.

Vaneetha Rendall-Risner writes in her book *The Scars That Have Shaped Me: How God Meets Us in Suffering*, "This is the most precious answer God can give us: wait. It makes us cling to Him rather than to an outcome. God knows what I need; I do not. He sees the future; I cannot. His perspective is eternal; mine is not. He will give me what is best for me when it is best for me" (80, 2016).

Reread that quote from Rendall-Risner again. Then take a few minutes to meditate upon it. How do you feel about *wait* being the best answer that we can receive from God? Do you now have a different perspective of waiting?

_____

_____

_____

_____

Lesson 3: What to Do While We Wait

You did not think we would leave you without some practical application steps, did you? This was one of our biggest questions as well. What do we do while we wait? Thankfully, God did not leave that one unanswered either! Do you remember us telling you about active waiting and passive waiting? (Hint: It's back in the intro to chapter 3). You have a choice of which type of waiting you wish to engage.

Bishop David A. Hadley, Sr., in a devotional called *Strong Faith*, wrote "But one thing is certain: Before God moves suddenly, we will wait. Waiting for answers is a fact of life—nobody gets out of it. So, the question is not if we'll wait, but rather how we'll wait. And I believe how we wait will determine how long we wait" (Hadley, 2019). Refer back to the story of the Israelites and their journey through the desert. It took them 40 years to actually reach the land God had promised to them. The journey would not have taken so long, had they actively waited upon the Lord. Instead, the Israelites give us a perfect example of waiting badly.

They started out well, praising the Lord for their deliverance from the Egyptians. Exodus 14:5–31 tells the story of Moses leading the Israelites to the edge of the sea and God saving them by parting the sea and allowing them to cross. Then, in Exodus 15:1–18, we read the praise song that the people sang to God in response. However, they soon lost their faith in God's promise. They blatantly began to disobey God. We read in Exodus 32 the story of the golden calf that they created to worship instead of God. The people said that they were unsure of what happened to Moses and that they needed other gods to go before them. In Numbers 11:4–6, the Israelites complained about not having what they **wanted** to eat, even though the Lord was providing all that they needed. In Numbers 14, the rebellion continues, and they complain about being in the wilderness and their fear of being killed by their enemies. They lost sight of God's PROMISE of freedom in the land of milk and honey because they would not actively wait on Him. This promise came with the guarantee that their enemies would fall if they would put their trust in Him. We can learn from their mistakes and do better for ourselves.

We can assure you God **will** answer you. He desires to answer you. He also desires for you to grow in character and place yourself in a posture of dependence on Him.

So, back to the question. What can you do while you wait? God gives us the answer. First, we choose to wait expectantly, not passively or begrudgingly. Listed below are some of the things that we can do during those times.

1. **Seek the Lord**—Actively seeking God might look different for different people. The one thing that we all must do when we seek Him is to genuinely ask Him to enter this time of waiting with us. How do we seek Him?

a. <u>Spend time in the Word studying, pursuing answers, and claiming God's promises.</u> There are multiple ways to accomplish this. A *word study* is focusing on a specific word and what it means throughout Scripture. You can do a *topical study* by selecting a specific theme and tracking it through the Bible. *Verse-mapping* is another way to learn about God's Word. Verse-mapping involves looking up the definitions of the words in a specific verse and applying the meaning to your life. Some people enjoy *character studies* where they learn about a particular person from the Bible. Another way is to study one of the books of the Bible.

We know that God's Word is trustworthy and will help to guide us. Proverbs 30:5 says, "Every word of God is flawless; He is a shield to those who take refuge in Him," while 2 Timothy 3:16–17 tells us, "All Scripture is God-breathed and is useful for teaching, rebuking, correcting and training in righteousness, so that the servant of God may be thoroughly equipped for every good work."

b. Spend time in prayer praying about the issues, praying for wisdom and discernment, AND praying for others. Prayer is our direct line for speaking to and hearing from God. When we pray, He hears us and He also answers. Read 1 John 5:14: "This is the confidence we have in approaching God: that if we ask anything according to His will, He hears us." We can wait expectantly knowing that we are heard by God. "Ask, and it will be given to you, seek, and you will find; knock, and it will be opened to you" (Matthew 7:7). We also grow closer to Him when we pray because we get to know His character even better.

c. Spend time meditating on who God is, what He is wanting to do in us and through us, and on what we need to do by way of answers and direction. While it is important to pray and to read His Word, it is also imperative that we sit in silence and listen for the Lord. Being silent can allow us to hear His voice and can allow the Holy Spirit to help us. "In the same way, the Spirit helps us in our weakness. We do not know what we ought to pray for, but the Spirit Himself intercedes for us through wordless groans. And He who searches our hearts knows the mind of the Spirit, because the Spirit intercedes: for God's people in accordance with the will of God" (Romans 8:26–27).

2. **Trust in God**—This is where the Israelites went wrong. They did not trust in God. They wanted immediate results instead of relying on God to provide for them. We cannot have it our way, all the time. When we wait on God, we need to TRUST. God always keeps His promises, so we need to have faith and continue to rely on Him. We need to trust in HIS timing, HIS provisions, and HIS love for us. He even tells us that we cannot comprehend His ways. "'For My thoughts are not your thoughts, neither are your ways My ways,' declares the Lord. 'As the heavens are higher than the earth, so are My ways higher than your ways and My thoughts than your thoughts'" (Isaiah 55:8–9). We have no idea about the wonderful and awesome things He has in store for us. But to receive those things, we must wait.

3. **Have the Right Attitude**—While we wait for answers, life goes on. We still get up every day, interact with others, and make many small decisions. Since we know that answers from God are not always immediate, what should our daily lives look like? We need to make the choice to have the *correct attitude*. This means that we choose joy over negativity. We choose to resolve conflicts calmly, instead of getting irate. We choose to be grateful, instead of complaining.

We need to do what we can to keep God's Word in our hearts so that we can maintain a disposition that is pleasing to the Lord. We allow God to use the pause in our life to grow and change us. We choose to serve others in a way that will honor God, whether big or small.

Waiting correctly is an essential part of abiding in Christ. If you are abiding, the waiting is much less of a burden or struggle. Read Psalm 27:14 (NKJV), "Wait on the Lord; be of good courage, and He shall strengthen your heart; Wait, I say, on the Lord!"

If you have been waiting for God to answer a prayer, take a moment to check yourself. Are you actively waiting? Are there ways you can find to abide more closely in our Heavenly Father? If so, what are they? Write your thoughts here.

_____

_____

_____

_____

Here is a short prayer about waiting that you can pray as often as you need. Do not feel that this is all you can say though. Make the prayer your own and be honest with God about what you need.

> *Lord,*
>
> *I know and trust that You have plans to prosper me and to help me. While I know that Your ways are always best, sometimes I want immediate results. Forgive me for getting impatient and wanting to rush Your answers. When those thoughts try to overtake my mind, help me to remember to turn to You. Please do not allow me to settle for less than Your best for me. Remind me that You will come to me in the waiting and that what You have planned for me is better than anything I can ever imagine.*

Thank you, God, for giving me the best gift of all, You.

Amen.

Wow! That was intense. We pray that you have gained as much from completing this study as we have in the writing process. Did you have any holy freight trains run over you throughout this study?

May God bless you today and always.

BIBLIOGRAPHY

Abraham, L. "Weekly Devotional: Fruit of the Spirit—Self-Control." Grand Canyon University. https://www.gcu.edu/blog/spiritual-life/weekly-devotional-fruit-spirit-self-control#:~:text=2%20Timothy%201%3A7%20says,that%20is%20honorable%20to%20God.v.

Beliefnet.com. "What Happens When We Worship." June 6, 2016. https://www.beliefnet.com/faiths/galleries/what-happens-when-we-worship.aspx#:~:text=%20What%20Happens%20When%20We%20Worship%20%201,changes%20our%20brain%20structure%20and%20our...%20More%20.

BibleStudyTools.com "Chrestotes." 2021. https://www.biblestudytools.com/lexicons/greek/nas/chrestotes.html.

Bickle, M. "Abiding in Christ: Cultivating Union with God." MikeBickle.org. June 6, 2016. https://mikebickle.org/watch/2014_07_20_0815_MSG_FCF https://backup.storage.sardius.media/file/akamaiBackup-ihopkc-103762/IHOP/85/163/20140719_Abiding_in_Christ_Cultivating_Union_with_God_Jn15.5.pdf.

CompellingTruth.org. "Longsuffering." 2021. https://www.compellingtruth.org/Bible-longsuffering.html.

Dictionary.com. "Gentle." 2021. https://www.dictionary.com/browse/gentle.

Dictionary.com. "Joy." 2021. https://www.dictionary.com/browse
/joy.

Dictionary.com. "Self-Control." 2021. https://www.dictionary.com
/browse/self-control.

Hadley, D. A., Sr. "Day 1. Strong Faith." MyBible.com. 2019. https://
my.bible.com/reading-plans/17039-strong-faith/day/4.

Keathley, J. H. "Waiting on the Lord." 2004. Bible.org. https://bible
.org/article/waiting-lord.

Lewis, A. "Self-Control vs Holy Spirit-Control." SlideShare.net. May
23, 2013. https://www.slideshare.net/ameerahlewis/self-contr
ol-vs-holy-spirit-control.

Morris, W. "Fruit of the Spirit: Gentleness." YouTube. June 16, 2019.
https://www.youtube.com/watch?v=M5UGRKDfPpU.

O'Day, G. R. "I Have Called You Friends." Baylor.edu. 2008. https://
www.baylor.edu/content/services/document.php/61118.pdf.

Piper, J. "The New Commandment of Christ: 'Love One Another as I
Have Loved You.' DesiringGod.org. August 4, 2021. https://
www.desiringgod.org/messages/the-new-commandment-of
-christ-love-one-another-as-i-have-loved-you.

Rendall-Risner, V., and J. Eareckson-Tada. *The Scars That Have
Shaped Me: How God Meets Us in Suffering*. Minneapolis,
MN: Desiring God, 2016.

Seale, N. "The Fruit of the Spirit—Joy." BeLoved.com. June 11,
2018. https://www.be-lovedbeloved.com/blog/2018/6/9/fruit
-of-the-spirit-joy.

Smyth, D. "The Four Types of Love in Scripture and How to
Experience Them Today." Crosswalk.com. April 17, 2020.
https://www.crosswalk.com/faith/bible-study/agape-storge
-phileo-and-eros-love-in-scripture.html.

Webster Dictionary. "Abide." 2014. http://www.webster-dictionary
.net/definition/abide.

Wilson, P. "The Spiritual Benefits of Waiting." FaithGateway.com. November 19, 2015. https://www.faithgateway.com/spiritual -benefits-waiting/#.YTPup51KiM-.

Witmer, S. "Kindness Changes Everything." DesiringGod.org. September 4, 2021. https://www.desiringgod.org/articles/kin dness-changes-everything.